THE SONY
VISION

THE SONY VISION

by Nick Lyons

Crown Publishers, Inc., New York

BOOKS BY NICK LYONS

Jones Very: Selected Poems (ed.)
The Seasonable Angler
Fisherman's Bounty (ed.)
Fishing Widows
The Sony Vision

Inquiries should be addressed to
Crown Publishers, Inc., One Park Avenue, New York, N.Y. 10016.

Published simultaneously in Canada by
General Publishing Company Limited

Printed in the United States of America

Designed by Shari de Miskey

Library of Congress Cataloging in Publication Data

Lyons, Nick.
The Sony vision. 5.5.

Bibliography: p. 225-230.
~~Includes index.~~

1. Soni Kabushiki Kaisha. 2. Electronic industries
—Japan—History. I. Title.
HD9696.A3J3636 1976   338.7'61'62130952   76-20703
ISBN 0-517-52739-1

*All photographs and drawings, except as
otherwise noted, courtesy Sony Corporation*

For

DICK FRIEDEN

who has tried strenuously
to instruct me in such matters
these past twenty-five years

Acknowledgments

Many people gave freely of their time and special knowledge to make this book possible. I am especially grateful to Akio Morita, Mrs. Akio Morita, Masaru Ibuka, Kazuo Iwama, Norio Ohga, Shigeru Kobayashi, Noboru Yoshii, Akio Ohkoshi, Senri Miyaoka, Mitsuru Ohki, Hajime Unoki, Hiroshi Yamakawa, Kazuo Sekino, Seiji Hayashida, Masahiko Morizono, Dr. Makoto Kikuchi, Heitaro Nakajima, Masaaki Morita, Nobutoshi Kihara, Yoshitoshi Araki, Akira Higuchi, Susumu Yoshida, Masao Kurahashi, Ryuichi Baba, Yasumitsu Watanabe, Dr. Michio Hatoyama, Kazuya Miyatake, Shokichi Suzuki, and other members of Sony in Japan.

Mike Morimoto and Ron Dishno in San Diego and, in New York, Harvey Schein, Kenneth Nees, Ray Steiner, Irving Sagor, Mort Fink, Hiroko Onoyama, Ira Morais, K. Hiramatsu, Sumio Sano, and Michael Schulhof were helpful. Philip Goodman of L. F. Rothschild and Robert Czepiel of Cyrus J. Lawrence, along with several other analysts, gave me the benefit of their special perspective.

Nobuyoshi Fukuda, of the executive office of Sony in Tokyo, was extremely helpful to me during my visit to Japan —and a great aid in gathering the photographs used in this book. The book would have been quite impossible without the constant aid of Sen Nishiyama, who is more thoroughly acknowledged elsewhere. Edward F. Rosiny not only served the indispensable role of "go-between" but gave me constant support and encouragement. Herbert Michelman again proved himself a most thoughtful and discerning editor, and Ann Cahn a sensitive copy editor.

Contents

Prologue

RESEARCHING AND writing this book has been a revelation.

I could not have begun a project with more misgivings: I am neither a scientist nor a management expert; I knew nothing about Japan; though I studied business as an undergraduate, I switched with a vengeance to the humanities—in fact, I never quite understood that hiatus in Industry 101 between the days when an immigrant kid delivered telegrams faster than anyone else and then, miraculously, became Andrew Carnegie. Nor was I sure I wanted to understand. Frankly, I had become more interested in how Yeats got from Innisfree to Byzantium. It seemed a more human concern.

But for many years I had in the back of my mind the thought of doing one corporate chronicle—what led to the company's growth, what people and what human factors limned its history, how the firm affected the world in which I lived. The corporate world is seen too blithely, too blindly as a corporate jungle: I wanted to explore one of its best examples, as I might explore a stretch of an unknown river, to understand it better. Also, when this book was suggested to me I had just finished reading Saul Bellow's *Humboldt's Gift,* and had been brooding on his speculations that "poets like drunkards and misfits or psychopaths" sank into weakness, perhaps because they had "no transforming knowledge comparable to the knowledge of Boeing or Sperry Rand or IBM or RCA." Sony was not such a giant but it would do just fine; in fact, its thirty-year history was more cohesive; I had hints that it valued innovation and creativity and freedom—which, in other contexts, I surely valued—and that it embodied rare business and scientific genius, which I wanted to understand.

What "transforming knowledge" did Sony possess?
By what means—fair or foul—was it got?
Who were the people responsible for its growth?
What did its products augur for the world?

I knew that the brilliant Japanese novelists Kawabata and Mishima, both suicides, had fought precisely the rise of industrialism in Japan that Sony's growth paralleled. Certainly I did not want to write a hymn to such industrialization; but I did want to know it better. I believed then, and believe now, that we must be fitfully careful lest the railroads ride us and television—even Trinitrons—teach us not to see.

I was intensely curious. Could a corporate profile be engaging as human drama? What values would emerge?

I insisted that the publisher, not the company, fund the book; neither had desired otherwise: Sony has not controlled or sponsored the writing of this book. But I also wanted, before anything else, assurances that I could explore at will and that Sony would give me free access to whomever I chose to see. I was startled when such permission was granted without hesitation. Three or four Sony executives even remarked that I should scrutinize their firm with great care; I should be coldly objective, and they would value such an outsider's view. I was impressed.

As I continued my research and interviews, I was delighted to realize that I had found a company whose story did not depend upon the discovery of warts to make it interesting. Sony's history is dramatic and unique; it has not happened before and could surely not happen in the future. Other Japanese and American companies have startling growth cycles—but none embody the special ingredients I found here. This is not the story of quick riches but of extraordinary vision, effort, and business genius. Kazuo Iwama, the new president of Sony, sent a revealing message to employees throughout the world in January 1976. He reaffirmed that from the beginning one basic concept had guided the company: "to contribute to human society by developing new products of excellent quality and performance, which are then offered through newly pioneered markets."

Sony has lived this concept—and given the lie to Carnegie's cold assertion that "pioneering doesn't pay."

Since I do not speak a word of Japanese, readers may be concerned about the reliability of my interviews, and the many quotes that appear in this book. Some are from English-speaking Japanese, others are not. In Sen Nishiyama, my constant companion in Japan, I was blessed not only with a translator fully bilingual and bicultural—a former United States Embassy adviser who, Frank Gibney says, "has probably interpreted more important conferences, business and diplomatic, than almost anyone in Japan"—but also the author of the recent book *Understanding and Misunderstanding,* a study of Japanese-American linguistic relations. To compound my good fortune, Sen Nishiyama is also a trained scientist. Despite the wealth of impressions he shared with me, and the many books I have read on the subject, I have avoided the temptation to write about Japanese culture and business in general, except where it directly revealed aspects of the Sony operation; other authors—like Gibney, Richard Halloran, Herman Kahn, Chie Nakane, Takeo Doi—have written superior books on these subjects. This book is merely the story of one maverick corporation based in Japan.

I began this project in a large spare office on the forty-third floor of 9 West Fifty-seventh Street in New York City, a room with an unobstructed view of Central Park through vast, nearly floor-to-ceiling windows. There was a striking Dubuffet, vintage 1955, on the wall, and behind the large desk a silver-haired man who was warm, witty, and commanding. The man was Akio Morita; he and Masaru Ibuka had founded Sony thirty years earlier in a bombed-out department store several months after the Japanese surrender. When I later asked Ibuka, innocently, what in brief was different about Sony, he gave a light laugh and said, in English, "everything."

Writing this book has given me a glimpse into the meaning of that word, into the heart of a major multinational; it has enabled me to travel across the world, to San Diego, Tokyo, Nagoya, and Fukuoka, and to visit plants and offices and speak to many remarkable men. Studying the vision that enabled Sony to get from the ash heaps of postwar Tokyo to that spacious New York office—and elsewhere—has surely been a revelation.

It is also a most human concern.

—Nick Lyons
May 1976

Brief Sony Highlights

BRIEF SONY HIGHLIGHTS . . . .

1945 October. Tokyo Tsushin Kenkyusho (Tokyo Telecommunications Laboratory) established by Masaru Ibuka

1946 May. Tokyo Tsushin Kogyo K.K. (Tokyo Telecommunications Engineering Corporation) formally incorporated by Ibuka and Akio Morita

1950. August. Marketed the first magnetic recording tape and tape recorder in Japan

1952 December. Developed the stereophonic audio system for the first stereophonic broadcasting in Japan through NHK

1953 August. Introduced the vidicon TV camera

1954 May. First successful production of transistors in Japan

1955 August. Marketed the first all-transistor radio, TR-55, in Japan
November. Marketed the first home-use stereophonic tape recorder, TC-551, in Japan

1957 March. Marketed the world's first pocket-size all-transistor radio, TR-63

1958 January. Adopted the trade name Sony for its corporate name

October. Received the Gold Medal Prize at the Brussels World's Fair for its power transistor and photo transistor

December. Developed the first transistorized video tape recorder in Japan

1959 June. Unveiled the successful development of the Esaki Tunnel Diode, a revolutionary semiconductor device for which Esaki eventually shared the Nobel Prize in Physics

December. Introduced the world's first all-transistor direct-view 8-inch television

1960 February. Established Sony Corporation of America

1961 June. Opened the Sony Research Center in Yokohama; publicly offered 2 million shares of Sony common stock in the form of ADRs in the United States—the first stock offering of a Japanese company in America

1962 April. Introduced the world's smallest and lightest all-transistor 5-inch Micro-TV

1963 March. Introduced the world's first all-transistor portable video tape recorder for industrial use

1964 September. Introduced the Sony Chromatron Color TV

November. Introduced the world's first home-use all-transistor video tape recorder

1965 August. Marketed the world's first home-use video tape recorder

1966 April. Opened the new Sony building in the Ginza

November. Introduced the world's first integrated circuit radio

1968 February. CBS-Sony joint venture established in Japan
April. Developed the Trinitron color television picture tube

1969 May. Compact Cassette-Corder taken aboard the Apollo 10 spaceship on its successful mission to the moon
October. Announced the Sony color video cassette system

1970 September. Sony's American depository shares were listed on the New York Stock Exchange—a first for a Japanese firm

1971 January. Developed the Trinicon, prototype model of color television camera with a single pickup tube
December. Ground broken for the San Diego color television plant

1972 January. Developed the new color video projection system, which projects video and television pictures on large display screens over 60 inches
March. Introduced the U-Matic video cassette system
July. Established Sony Trading Corporation, a worldwide importing firm

1975 May. Marketed the Betamax VTR

THE SONY VISION

CHAPTER ONE

On the Third-and Seventh-Floors

If it were possible to establish conditions where persons could become united with a firm spirit of teamwork and exercise to their hearts' desire their technological capacity . . . then such an organization would bring untold pleasure and untold benefits. . . . The war's end has speeded up the possibility of realizing this dream.

—MASARU IBUKA, FROM
"PROSPECTUS FOR ESTABLISHING
TOKYO TSUSHIN KOGYO," 1946

S ALES OF Sony products reached a high of $1,338,595,000 in 1975. Its trademark was registered in more than 170 countries and territories, and its name was a household word throughout the world. Sony had factories in America, the United Kingdom, Germany, and elsewhere, more than 20,000 employees, dozens of subsidiaries, and its stock was listed on

1

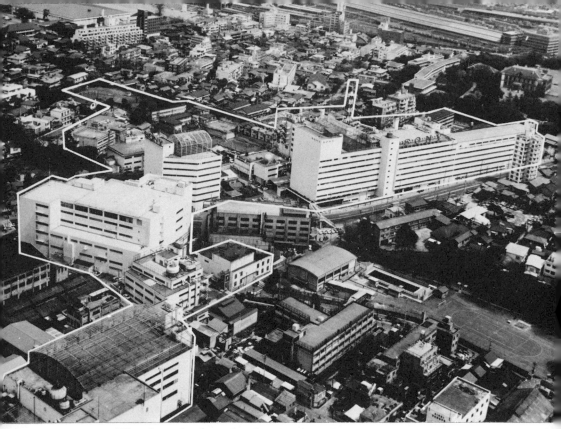

The Sony headquarters buildings (within the white outline) in Tokyo today.

all the major stock exchanges. In its first thirty years of operation, the company had pioneered and successfully introduced dozens of new electronic products into Japan and the world— tape recorders, the transistor radio, the microtelevision, the unique Trinitron color tube, the Betamax video tape-recording unit—and had established an enviable reputation for quality.

Last year was also a time of challenge. The plummeting economy hit the electronics industry with special ferocity. Earnings fell—a precedent in Sony's history. But when people began to speak of the "myth of Sony," Akio Morita loudly proclaimed that there had never been a myth.

Still, the story of Sony has all the elements of a myth—or at least a novel. Its growth has been phenomenal. In its first year, sales were merely $6,944 and its profit $278; by the end of 1946, it employed a scant thirty-five people.

The firm now known as Sony began in a small corner room

on the third floor of the burned-out, blackened, and nearly empty Shirokiya department store on Tokyo's Ginza, several weeks after the war ended. The room, which had been the switchboard area for the store, had a few old desks, one old sofa-type chair, a hot plate, and some meager electronics equipment and materials; the windows, which had been broken during the bombings, were at first boarded over; the rent was negligible. The devastating results of Curtis LeMay's B-29s, flying low and dropping napalm-filled M47 fire bombs on Tokyo in the spring and summer of 1945, were everywhere apparent. The city was a flattened gray shambles. More than thirty-four square miles, 65 percent of the city, were reduced to cinders. The gutted, windowless shells of a few hardy buildings, their bare ferroconcrete walls charred and rutted, stood bleakly amid the gray rubble; former industrial plants were mazes of charred steel girders. In the streets one could see only a few antiquated taxis and buses, like the old four-cylinder Datsun panel truck Ibuka bought for $100 and had to hand-crank to start. Food was scarce and sharply rationed, and there was widespread malnutrition; one Sony employee remembers weeks when he had only a single yam for lunch, or a handful of toasted soybeans. For warmth, the engineers had only a hot plate—and had to "wear plenty underneath." There were nearly 7 million Japanese soldiers to be demobilized, and the per capita income that year would stand only slightly over $17.

Masaru Ibuka, a lean, soft-spoken man of thirty-seven, had come to Tokyo with seven young engineers to start some sort of electronics laboratory or enterprise. He had been chief engineer for Japan Precision Instrument Co., his own private measuring-instruments company during the war, supplying the military with vacuum-tube voltmeters and a variety of other precision instruments, and he felt an obligation to provide work for his men. Electric and mechanical companies had traditionally been separate, but he had brooded on how to combine them. During the war telephone conversations in China were being monitored, and Ibuka developed an audio frequency generator that, at 2,000 cycles, could be applied to a telephone system to ensure privacy of conversation. The military bought this and, further interested in his theories, encouraged him to design a thermo-guidance system for bombs that would direct themselves to a source of heat; the system never reached completion, but during the project he met Akio Morita, a skinny twenty-three-year-old naval lieutenant, a trained physicist, who would later join his little firm in Tokyo. When the bombings started, Ibuka, like many other small subcontractors that supplied the military, moved to the country; he chose to set up shop 125 miles across the island, in Nagano Prefecture, and elected an apple orchard for a site, "so we would at least have apples to eat." Then, in late August 1945, taking what few measuring instruments and material he could, and seven young engineers, with his total savings about $1,600, he headed for Tokyo.

Ibuka's immediate need was to find some means of providing for the group, and at first they considered all sorts of bizarre enterprises: trying to sell sweetened bean-paste soup, building miniature golf equipment, making slide rules.

After the war the Japanese were hungry for music and for news of the world; many had war-damaged radios or radios that had had the shortwave unit disconnected by the military police (so they couldn't tune in on enemy propaganda). Ibuka and his men—often well into the night—repaired radios, made shortwave converters for medium-wave sets, then expanded to produce phonograph pickup units. They had the equipment and also some old contacts for vacuum-tube voltmeter production; this became a mainstay that first autumn, when food was so scarce they would have to take rucksacks and go out into the countryside, to farms, to buy potatoes and rice—and then dodge the police because rice was strictly controlled. Often Ibuka paid most of the salaries out of his own small and dwindling savings; the men would have worked that autumn merely for food.

Below them, on the first floor, the department store began

to refurbish its counters, stock what meager goods it could acquire; its tiny radio section began to get repair orders and soon it combined forces with Ibuka's team and arranged for them to handle all this work. Akira Higuchi, one of those first seven engineers and later a deputy president of Sony, remembers making house calls to repair larger sets. Ibuka also began to get contracts and orders for odd jobs in electronics from the Ministry of Communications, with which he had had contact during the war.

Though they did not precisely have a flourishing business, within a few months they needed more room and found space on the seventh floor of the same eight-story building, beside a little movie theatre and a barbershop. The second floor of the building and the third, fourth, fifth, and sixth floors held nothing: They were merely gutted black rooms connected by a rickety staircase.

Ibuka had clear, even idealistic objectives, but no concrete idea of what he wanted to make. He especially wanted to apply that mix of electronics and engineering to the consumer field. But with what products? "Our first major momentum," he recalls, "began with the realization that we were not a group of people who could compete with the companies already in existence, against products in which they specialized. We started with the basic concept that we had to do something that no other company had done before." Since he wanted to make merchandise needed in daily life, and realized that there was a severe shortage of fuel but some electricity, one of his first developments was an electric rice cooker.

He bought a number of those small wooden tubs in which hot rice is put and, in place of the wooden bottom, installed an electric heater. The principle was simple. Two spiral-shaped pieces of aluminum were connected, interlocked, on the bottom; when water was added and 100 volts AC of electricity applied, the water heated and then, at the proper temperature, automatically stopped. "It was a very good idea," muses Ibuka with a light laugh, "but . . . *but!*" The result, unfortunately, depended upon the kind of rice used and the weight of the water. Sometimes very tasty rice was produced, sometimes not. They soon had an inventory of over a hundred of these ingenious wooden tubs and were unable to sell them. Not one.

Akio Morita was born in 1921 in Nagoya, the first son of Kyuzaemon Morita, the fourteenth-generation head of a prominent sake brewing and distributing house carrying the prestige brand name "Neno-hi-matsu"; the firm could trace its business back to the seventeenth century. From the time Akio was in the third grade, Kyuzaemon often took him to the head office of the firm, where the boy was required to watch his father work, learn something of balance sheets and market strategy, and stand by his father's side when the elder Morita spoke to a general assembly of employees. By tradition, the boy was expected to become the fifteenth-generation head of Morita Company, Ltd.

But as he grew, Akio became more and more interested in science. He tinkered with and learned to fix all sorts of mechanical objects, and in the first year of junior high school experimented with piano wire to make a primitive magnetic recording device. In his early love of experimentation, he was like Ibuka (the descendant of a leading samurai family), who as a boy built elaborately complex structures with Mecano sets, disassembled his grandfather's watch (and couldn't reassemble it), dismantled an electric bell and then rigged a local telegraph system to a neighboring friend's house, became a radio ham, and, later, started to take apart an acetylene bicycle headlight—which exploded in his hands. Ibuka was less delighted with the fact that his fingers weren't blown off than with the phenomenon of the explosion.

Ibuka, determined to follow an electrical engineering career in what was then known as "weak currents" (electronics), went to Waseda University; while there he developed a system of transmitting sound by modulating a neon light, for which he received a patent and then an award in an international exhibition in Paris. Though he showed great talent for invention, he failed the employment examination for the Tokyo-Shibaura Electric Company, and only through the intervention of a friend from the patent office finally found his first job with the Photo-Chemical Laboratory Company, a motion-picture film recording and processing firm that also produced movies. When PCL became exclusively a production company, Ibuka got himself transferred to an affiliate that produced vacuum tubes and, eventually, electronic instruments.

By the time Morita entered Osaka Imperial University in 1940, he had committed himself to science—though his father, thinking this interest was a "hobby," still fully expected him to join the sake firm. He studied under Professor Tsunesaburo Asada, a well-known physicist who wrote a weekly column on science for the *Asahi Shimbun;* Morita, one of his best students, sometimes ghosted the articles. Japan was already entangled in the global crisis when Morita started at Osaka, and when he graduated in March 1944, he joined the navy as a cadet technical officer. There are reports that even in that tense last year of the war, Morita gained a quick reputation for getting things done, for cutting a broad swath through bureaucratic red tape. One story has him saving sake rations (he dislikes all drinking) and, in 1944, hosting an elaborate party for an admiral he wanted to impress.

Morita's specialty was electronics, and he was sufficiently promising by now to attend meetings in Yokohama of the secret wartime Research Committee. Through the committee, he met Ibuka and later visited him in Nagano Prefecture, where they studied the possibilities of producing the thermal-guidance system and noctovision devices. Though Ibuka was more than a dozen years older, they became intimate friends.

In the chaos following the surrender, Morita returned to his home near Nagoya while his friend struggled with the tiny shop in Tokyo. Ibuka's shortwave adapters attracted enough attention for the October 6 edition of the *Asahi Shimbun* to carry an article on this project, mentioning Ibuka's name.

Morita read the column and immediately wrote to his friend, who replied at once, urging the younger man to come to Tokyo; he valued Morita's friendship and natural enthusiasm, but also—because his money was beginning to run out—Morita represented a potential source of financing. Though Ibuka couldn't guarantee much of a salary, he readily conveyed the mission he felt to make their technology available in peacetime Japan.

But Morita also received a letter from one of his former professors, now teaching at the Tokyo Institute of Technology, offering him a job as a lecturer. Morita decided to teach—but agreed to work part time in Ibuka's shop.

During the war, whenever Ibuka received orders from the military, they supplied the parts and materials needed to complete the work; otherwise, few were available. He had always wanted the general public to be the market for whatever he produced and felt locked in by this situation. After the war he determined to start with the materials themselves, which would give him full freedom. He had brought some technical equipment and parts from Nagano Prefecture; new material was at first unavailable but as the months wore on, parts and components from the dismantled Japanese military organization began to slip onto the market. With careful searching—sometimes in salvage piles or junkyards—he began to acquire what he wanted.

But what should his shop make?

They did not want to remain in the radio repair business. This was just a stopgap.

Making radios was a distinct possibility. They had the technical expertise and even the equipment to do this. But many other, and much larger, manufacturers were already producing radios and similar products; these firms had larger staffs, more advanced technology—they were already perhaps years ahead. Ibuka did not want to produce what the large manufacturers had the potential to produce. He wanted to find new areas, products that no other manufacturer had even conceived of.

Meanwhile, Douglas MacArthur issued a fateful order. All former high officials in the Japanese government, top executives from the *zaibatsu* (the vast holding companies), and former military officers were officially banned, in what became known as "The Purge," from holding public office. This included teaching. Morita, a former naval lieutenant, was forced to leave the classroom.

This proved a fortuitous stroke.

As an outside member, Morita had been helping Ibuka in the shop. When his lectureship was terminated, he had the option of joining Ibuka full time or finally entering his father's well-established sake and soy sauce company. Ibuka immediately went by night train to Nagoya; the windows on the train were broken and he was nearly frozen by the time he got there the next morning, but he had come on an important mission: He wanted to meet with Morita's father and convince him that his son should join the struggling firm. The elder Morita was at first not impressed. In fact, even several years later he tried to dissuade some of his son's friends from entering or investing in the firm, saying they would be crazy to do so. Yet, he not only agreed to Ibuka's requests but even began to invest his company's funds in the little electronics firm—and eventually became Sony's largest stockholder.

Morita and Ibuka were impeccably consonant.

The special genius that would fully develop in each man in later years required the other as catalyst to bring it to fruition; the weaknesses of one were counterbalanced by the strengths of the other. Ibuka, quietly passionate about his innovations, tenacious in research and development, a humanist in management policies, was something of a dreamer; Morita, a trained and able physicist, was always a realist—and even more valuable, he would soon be forced to develop his talents as a brilliant financier and marketing link to the outside world;

he was already a dervish, animated and persuasive. "Ibuka is such a warm and honest person," says Morita, "that I saw at once that I had to become tough and shrewd to protect him. My mission became to realize Ibuka's dream." One early employee, with obviously deep affection for Ibuka, said Ibuka alone would surely have failed: "He had hardly any interest in adding sums. There is something childlike about the man." But "Morita alone would not have had that special variety of new products to sell. Though they are diametrically different, Morita is one of the few people who fully understands Ibuka—and has been able to *harmonize* his genius. They are the closest of friends." They would develop total confidence in each other, and the inside direction of Ibuka would be given the fullest exposure to the world by Morita.

"When Morita came," one engineer from the early days told me, "that was the beginning."

Within a few months, on May 7, 1946, they incorporated as the Tokyo Tsushin Kogyo Kabushiki Kaisha—Tokyo Telecommunications Engineering Co., Ltd. Since there were government regulations making it difficult for a company capitalized at over 200,000 yen to incorporate, they listed their paid-up capital at 198,000 yen—variously converted to $500 or $600. The figure, which has come down in legend as the actual funds of the firm, was not much of an exaggeration. The company had about twenty employees.

The prospectus establishing Tokyo Telecommunications, composed by Ibuka, is a remarkable document. It shows foresight and rare concern for the human factor in industry. It has been a guiding force for the company these past thirty years, modified only slightly as it grew with extraordinary speed and, in 1950, became a publicly listed corporation.

"Those of like minds have naturally come together," the prospectus says, to embark on these ideals "at the same time that the New Japan has begun." Among the specific "Purposes of Incorporation," Ibuka vowed:

- The establishment of an ideal factory—free, dynamic, and pleasant—where technical personnel of sincere motivation can exercise their technological skills to the highest levels.

- Dynamic activities in technology and production for the reconstruction of Japan and the elevation of the nation's culture.

- Prompt application of the highly advanced technology developed during the war in various sectors to the life of the general public.

- Making rapidly into commercial products the superior research results of universities and research institutes, which are worth applying to the daily lives of the public.

八、録字通信機

A page from the original prospectus, drafted by Ibuka and presented hand-inscribed—since the company did not own a typewriter.

A Tokyo Tsushin Kogyo vacuum-tube voltmeter, from a 1949 catalog; this product was the mainstay in the company's earliest years.

When Ibuka wrote this, Tokyo Telecommunications had only produced the ill-fated electric rice cooker, vacuum-tube voltmeters, shortwave converters, and a random assortment of assigned technical products for the rapidly burgeoning communications industry; their finances were so low that the old Datsun truck—which only Ibuka and Morita could drive, making all deliveries and pickups themselves—had to be sold; even the banks, so central to the growth of so many Japanese businesses after the war, were reluctant to lend the company short-term money, so operating funds were constantly begged from family and friends, especially Morita's father.

The "Management Policies" of the new firm were equally unusual. They included these vows:

- We shall eliminate any untoward profit-seeking, shall constantly emphasize activities of real substance, and shall not seek expansion of size for the sake of size.

- Rather, we shall seek a compact size of operation through which the path of technology and business activities can advance in areas that large enterprises, because of their size, cannot enter.

- We shall be as selective as possible in our products and will even welcome technological difficulties. We shall focus on highly sophisticated technical products that have great usefulness in society, regardless of the quantity involved. Moreover, we shall avoid the formal demarcation between electricity and mechanics, and shall create our own unique products coordinating the two fields, with a determination that other companies cannot overtake.

- Utilizing to the utmost the unique features of our firm, which shall be known and trusted among the acquaintances in the business and technical worlds, we shall open up through mutual cooperation our production and sales channels and our acquisition of supplies to an extent equal to those of large business organizations.

- We shall guide and foster subcontracting factories in directions that will help them become independently operable and shall strive to expand and strengthen the pattern of mutual help with such factories.

- Personnel shall be carefully selected, and the firm shall be comprised of as small a number as feasible. We shall avoid mere formal position levels and shall place our main emphasis on ability, performance, and personal character, so that each individual can show the best in ability and skill.

There was little enough to "manage" at first. The men working at benches on the seventh floor were highly motivated;

often, on their own, they worked late into the night and on weekends. Morita and Ibuka had calculated that if they could make ten vacuum-tube voltmeters a month, this would be enough to pay the salaries; by December 1946, they were making thirty to forty. Ibuka, constantly experimenting, developed an electrically heated cushion, and they sold several hundred of these—though several senior employees doubt if it would have been approved by the Underwriters' Laboratory.

Slowly the skill and reliability of the firm was becoming known.

Through Ibuka's contacts, orders came in from the National Railways and other governmental agencies and from Japan Broadcasting (NHK). They sold fifty vacuum-tube voltmeters to the Ministry of Communications, then worked on a resonator sound generator to replace the old clicking telegraph sound. Most of the communications people, who had served in the Japanese Signal Corps, were not accustomed to the clicking code, and when they were discharged and working for various communications services, they were unable to recognize this kind of sound. So Ibuka developed a resonator that mechanically joined a carbon microphone and a small loudspeaker; when an impulse or code came into the microphone, this activated the loudspeaker, which in turn created an acoustic circuit back into the microphone, producing short and long tones for the dots and dashes rather than the clicks.

The department store began to expand its business, to repair its gutted building, and install merchandise on the other floors; on the seventh floor, where Tokyo Telecommunications did most of its actual production, a cabaret was preparing to start operations—and all day the workers could hear partitions being torn down, and singers and dancers auditioning. Though housing of all kinds throughout the city was extremely scarce, it was time to move.

At first they took space in several widely separated locations—one on a floor above Ketel's, a German restaurant on the Ginza, another in the west part of Tokyo, in facilities owned

Probably the earliest photograph in Sony's files, soon after the firm moved from the department store to a series of shacks. *From left to right:* Akira Higuchi, Masaru Ibuka, Kazuo Iwama, and an unidentified worker.

An early company photograph, taken inside the Tokyo Tsushin workshop, probably by Morita.

by the Yokogawa Electric Company. But this split proved extremely inconvenient. Finally, in 1947, through the owner of a shop that electroplated the tuning forks needed for Ibuka's telegraph resonator, they acquired some old shacks in the Shinegawa area; these were so dilapidated that during a rainstorm the executives had to work with umbrellas over their desks. But in time they added more buildings to this complex, then tore them down, and eventually built the present headquarters for Sony on this site.

Contracts from NHK became increasingly important to the struggling firm. Much broadcasting equipment had been destroyed during the war, other equipment required delicate revision, and broadcasting was one of the most important areas of concern for the Occupation Forces. The Civil Information and Education section (CI & E) of the Occupation headquarters oversaw the entire industry and insisted that all systems throughout the country be revised to meet existing American standards.

When an especially large order from NHK came in for the production of a highly sophisticated mixer-console, an American officer was sent to the shack-factory in Shinegawa at which the company then worked. He was so dismayed by what he saw that he returned to NHK officials and severely berated them for placing such an important order with a tiny operation, one with hardly any significant products to show, shabby quarters, and a miniscule staff. News of this got back to Ibuka and he decided the firm should prove its worth. When Tokyo Telecommunications produced a highly competent console and delivered it precisely on time, the American officer was amazed —and impressed. From then on he saw that the Occupation Forces themselves placed orders with Ibuka for broadcasting equipment.

With increasing financial support from Morita's father, and more and more orders coming in daily, the firm was able to survive through the first three immensely difficult years following the surrender. Other firms were less successful. Many

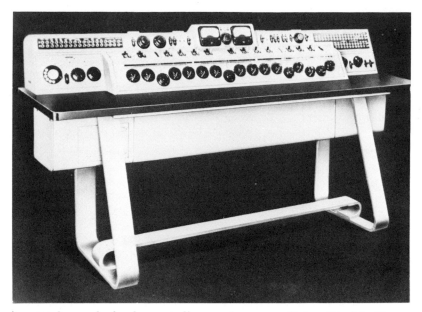

A control console for large studios, an important Tokyo Tsushin Kogyo product in the late 1940s.

that had close connections with branches of the military, and were able to secure good quantities of silicon steel, aluminum ingots, and other important material easily in 1946 and 1947, but manufactured below government specifications or failed to develop their technology, went bankrupt. The mortality was high. But Tokyo Telecommunications insisted from the beginning on quality production, and continued to develop its technical capabilities. By 1948 it had only about seventy employees but through careful supervision of the work of the many subcontractors commonly used in Japanese industry, it was able to take on a considerable volume of business. By this time it was performing almost all the revision work to convert older equipment to current standards required by NHK throughout Japan.

But both Ibuka and Morita were dissatisfied.

They still did not have a unique consumer product.

This had been their initial dream. They had vowed to make that which other manufacturers did not or could not produce; they had wanted to manufacture for the general public. Instead, they were doing revision work for NHK, producing vacuum-tube voltmeters for commercial use, and a variety of other highly limited professional items—relay systems, variable filters, a megaphone, a tubeless interphone, push-button switches.

They considered the wire recorder.

Perhaps.

Excellent magnetic wire had been developed at one of the universities and Dr. Kenzo Nagai had invented a high frequency biasing system that was excellent for recording. Ibuka secured a Webster wire recorder and then he and a few of his best engineers began to study it carefully.

Perhaps.

This might be what they were looking for. It was unique and potentially a strong consumer product. They had the technological skill to produce the wire recorder. They were on the verge of committing their best resources to the production of such a machine when something happened that changed the entire direction of Tokyo Telecommunications.

One day, while visiting the CI & E office in the NHK building, a member of the Occupation Forces showed Ibuka a tape recorder.

CHAPTER TWO

999 Uses of the Tape Recorder

*We do not market a product that has been developed
already but develop a market for the product
we make.*

—AKIO MORITA

WHEN THEY began Tokyo Telecommunications, neither
Ibuka nor Morita had any consumer sales experience
whatsoever. Neither had taken a business administration or
marketing course in college, and neither had even produced a
significant consumer product. True, Ibuka had arranged various professional sales, and Morita might draw on what he could
remember from those random visits to his father's sake firm.
It was little enough. They both frankly admit that they believed
the world would beat a path to the door of their seedy factory,
that—should they develop the proper product—their fortune
was assured.

To the question "How to win the race?" both had already answered: "Choose an item in which we can use our specialty." They were electronics engineers. Their specialty was audio. "A swimmer," says Morita, "cannot win a marathon."

The tape recorder that Ibuka saw in the CI & E office had a tape speed of 7½ inches; it made very little noise and its sound quality was excellent. He was amazed at what the machine could do—and was immediately convinced that this was the product they had been looking for, the first major consumer product they should undertake, at whatever expense, to produce. Tape recorders were unheard of in Japan at the time. There wasn't even a name for them in the language and, like many other technical words, the foreign phrase was eventually incorporated with only phonetic adjustment.

The machine itself did not appear to pose serious problems. They checked the patents, discovered that Aditzo Electric held one for the invention by Dr. Nagai. They purchased the rights and knew they had the technical capacity in electric and magnetic circuitry to produce a good machine. The tape was another matter. They could find very little information about the tape, though it had been developed in Germany as early as 1937. Because of the war, little of the German technology had come into the United States, and until the Americans discovered that the Germans had such magnetic tape, the United States military had used wire recorders. Then, with information available after the war, Minnesota Mining and Manufacturing began to manufacture the tape and Ampex the recorder.

Ibuka and his engineers—including a new young man named Nobutoshi Kihara, who would have a distinguished career at Sony—knew that the magnetic material was a magnetic dust or powder; but they did not know how to produce the plastic base. In fact, there was absolutely no plastic in Japan at that time and, because of stringent import regulations, it was then virtually impossible to secure such a product.

What to do?

Cellophane was available, and that might serve as the tape

base. They had a lot of information on the magnetic materials and knew how to make the iron powder, but they quickly discovered that cellophane stretched and easily became distorted.

After months of intense experimentation, they decided to try paper. Morita had a cousin working in a paper manufacturing plant and they got him to prepare some high-quality calendered paper (sent through pressure rollers to give it a slick surface) for use as a possible tape base. This produced better results than cellophane but they learned that the paper would break easily if it caught even slightly in the machine; the engineers say this forced them to compensate, to take painstaking care in developing better circuitry, recording heads, and amplifiers for the tape recorder itself. They further improved their techniques of quality control by following concepts brought to Japan by Bell Laboratories engineers working in the Civil Communications section of the Occupation headquarters.

They had to develop the technique for producing the tape, then coating it with magnetic powder, all by themselves. There was no native technology available to them and they as yet had no way of obtaining reliable information from America, which none of them had visited.

It was a tremendous struggle. Worse, the whole effort was extraordinarily expensive, financially and in the commitment of personnel who might have been used elsewhere. Morita and Ibuka began a long, steady argument with their accounting manager, who trotted out the books and figures with increasing trepidation and kept warning them that they were spending far too much money: This dream could bankrupt the firm. "Just be a little more patient," Morita insisted, "and we will make a fortune." Throughout, they were buoyed by the prospect that once they produced a new item of high quality—like all the work they had already done for the broadcasting world —it would naturally sell.

In one section of the old warehouse building, where Morita worked with them, engineers began to design the various kinds of tape; in another, the recorder itself was being

The first factory and headquarters Sony built, on the same site it now occupies in Tokyo. The "T" stands for Tokyo Tsushin.

worked on; and in a small area on the same floor, the tapes themselves were made. At first, they would lay the paper out on the floor and then run back and forth with an airbrush, spraying on the magnetic powder. The engineers all laugh when they recall this primitive process. That would surely not do, so they tried other increasingly sophisticated methods of coating the paper and finally, after months of strenuous work, made an acceptable paper that could be mass-produced by coating it with iron oxide powder suspended in lacquer. They had designed the entire tape-coating machine themselves. Though this first paper tape had only about one-tenth the performance level of the tape produced by Minnesota Mining, they gradually improved the quality. Most important, they had made—by themselves—an auspicious start.

Ibuka and his chief engineers now credit the necessity to produce this rudimentary crude tape as the major impetus that enabled them to develop a broad range of technology. To this day Sony is one of the few electronics firms in the world with the capability of producing the entire range of audio equipment—from tapes to finished product. They have maintained the advantages of such repleteness in the world of video tape, which itself synthesizes the work of nearly a dozen different technologies.

By late 1949 they had managed to complete their first entire unit. The first pilot machine was very big, very heavy, and very expensive; this was followed quickly with the slightly more effective G-type tape recorder, the first in Japan. It weighed over one hundred pounds and would have to sell for the then enormous sum of 160,000 yen, about $400.

During the war, independently, two patents had been developed for the tape recorder—Dr. Nagai's in Japan, the other

The first G-type tape recorder.

in the United States. Each was, in effect, protected from the other because of the existing local patent. Tokyo Telecommunications could thus prevent any American tape recorders from entering Japan, because this would infringe upon the Japanese patent rights, which they now controlled; similarly, any Japanese tape recorder could be kept out of the United States. Until Morita went to America some years later to negotiate a contract with the patent holder there, whereby American tape recorders would be charged a royalty upon entering Japan (which Sony would collect as agent for the Japanese patent holder), and Sony tape recorders could enter the United States by paying a royalty, Sony had a virtual monopoly on the market. They were also years ahead of possible Japanese competitors in their technology, a situation they would later achieve many times with other new products. The first of their major risks seemed to have paid off: They had a unique product and an open market.

But would it sell?

Masao Kurahashi is a compact, vigorous, outgoing man; he thinks and speaks with speed and decision, and even in 1949 he would have been called a natural salesman. After the war he had been hired as managing director of a company called Yagumo Sangyo, which existed under the house of Tokugawa, descendants of the shogunate replaced by the Meiji Reformation. His principal job was to improve the company's finances. They were particularly searching for a viable consumer product to sell. Michiji Tajima, a director of Yagumo Sangyo, and also chairman of the board of Tokyo Telecommunications, suggested that Kurahashi consider the G-type Tape-corder. Ibuka and Morita, without any general sales experience and unable to market their new product, had recently decided to explore the possibility of having a sales agent or wholesaler handle their product for them.

As soon as Kurahashi saw the tape recorder demonstrated in the shabby warehouse-factory, he was tremendously interested. "We must be allowed to sell this for you!" he insisted.

He thought he could persuade the Tokugawa family to buy fifty for 6 million yen.

Morita and Ibuka were delighted. This was probably their first true sale of a product for consumer use. But there was another reason: They were capitalized at that time at 3.6 million yen and were extremely anxious to raise this to 10 million by the time they went public in 1950.

For three months Kurahashi tried every source, every method he could think of, but was unable to sell a single one of those fifty tape recorders. What was wrong? He was thoroughly sold on the product himself; he thought it was both interesting and original. And since he had persuaded Tokugawa to write a check for 6 million yen, he felt a tremendous responsibility for the purchase. After all, he had been hired to improve their finances.

He finally realized that the scores of prospective customers he visited did not know how to use this machine; worse, they didn't even know what use the tape recorder could be put to. In fact, *he* didn't even know its uses. Since Morita was not yet regularly involved in the public marketplace, he too was relying on Kurahashi to sell the machine. He had greatly appreciated the wholesale purchase of fifty, but what permanent value was that if no retail customers finally bought the tape recorder? Morita began to take a hard look at this marketing problem himself.

At last, after three months of strenuous work, Kurahashi sold his first unit—to an *oden* shop near Tokyo station. *Oden* is a special kind of food cooked in a soy sauce soup and served with sake. *Oden* shops are, in effect, like pubs, and after a few drinks the patrons often begin to talk loudly or sing. The proprietor would record someone's voice, then play it back. The patrons found it such marvelous entertainment that they came back in great numbers and told their friends.

Later, Kurahashi sold a second set to the Justice Ministry Branch Bureau in Nagoya for use in the courtroom. When the man in charge told him that "all the major branches should have this; it will be invaluable for court proceedings," he promptly went to the central office of the Justice Ministry and, six months after he had begun to sell the tape recorder, got a resounding order for sixty units. This looked like the beginning of something.

The sale of the *oden* shop had been a freak but when the Justice Ministry ordered so many for use in court, Kurahashi realized that someone had to have a definite use for the equipment before they would buy it. If he could get a prospective buyer to understand the particular use a tape recorder could be put to, the man would realize its value. With this in mind, he promptly sold some to the police to keep records of interrogation.

Morita, becoming more and more involved with consumer sales, came to the same realization one day after he had wandered by chance into an antiques shop. He saw curios, flower vases, fragile porcelain, knickknacks, crockery of various kinds; most of it did not seem particularly well shaped, and the prices seemed outrageously high. Since he had no particular interest in antiques, he was shocked when someone walked in and bought a carved ivory figurine Morita considered worthless— and exclaimed, when the sale was made, "What a bargain!"

Why had the man done it?

Why would someone spend their money on *this*, Morita thought, "when they could buy Japan's first tape recorder, a great technological achievement?"

And the price of the antique was *higher* than that of the tape recorder.

"I realized then," he recalls, "that a sale cannot be achieved unless a customer finds value in the merchandise. It must fill one of his needs." *He* did not "need" antiques; the other man obviously did. What then did selling actually consist of? "I reasoned," says Morita, "that to sell is to exchange what we have for the money in the pockets of other people. But how could we induce this customer to spend money out of his pocket? Pickpockets can get the money out—but we were not pickpockets." There was clearly a difference between the "scientific value" of his product and its value to the customer. *He* had not been educated to understand the value of the antiques and few people knew the value of a tape recorder. He and Kurahashi would have to learn the uses—as many as possible—and educate the public. Education was the necessary middle step. "*We* knew the value of our product," says Morita, "and had to have the confidence to convince others of its value *to them*. We were really in an *information* industry." In the future this became a fixed and seminal principle. Sony would produce innovative products; clearly they could not be truly innovative if everyone already knew their uses. Creativity in industry could not be brought to fruition without proper marketing. Without sales their fruits could not survive.

In its earliest hours Tokyo Telecommunications had vowed not to follow others but to pioneer new products: Now it had to learn to accept the further responsibility such creative technology would always demand. It had to sell to the public not so much a product but the new concept it had developed; it had to give the public a way of seeing its unrecognized and unfulfilled needs.

By accident, Kurahashi found an American pamphlet entitled "999 Uses of the Tape Recorder," an invaluable tool. He got the most important uses translated into Japanese and reproduced in a small sales booklet of his own (which still exists). By far the largest number of uses listed were in education. Astronomers and microbiologists, for instance, require both hands on the telescope or microscope; the tape recorder would be the best way to record their findings accurately while keeping both hands on their instruments.

In the late 1940s and early 1950s, the CI & E began to stress audiovisual education in Japan. Traditionally, Japanese education centered on reading, writing, and using the abacus; but the Americans insisted that it was also extremely important to learn to listen and to speak properly, particularly for the study of languages. At that time their only audiovisual tool was 16mm

The first page of the pamphlet listing 999 uses of the tape recorder, which
Kurahashi had translated into Japanese.

film, in English, which was distributed to film centers they
created in each of the prefectural headquarters. Ibuka and
Morita knew that with this concept being pressed upon Japanese
educators their tape recorder could become an extremely im-

portant tool. The Americans also encouraged NHK to develop school broadcasting programs that would be piped into the classrooms at designated times. But each school obviously had its own schedule and curriculum, which might well differ; and there were obvious disparities in the seasons: A special on cherry trees keyed to their brief blossoming period in Tokyo would scarcely coincide with that local event in Fukuoka to the south or Sapporo far north.

Ibuka and Morita realized that the G-type tape recorder was both too bulky and far too expensive for use in schools. But they had targeted their market now, and immediately retargeted their developmental engineering as well.

In surveying the price ranges that might be viable, they determined that a price of 60,000 to 70,000 yen, at the outset, would make it possible for schools to purchase their set. Ibuka brought all his top engineers together, then took all of them to Atami, a hot springs resort south of Yokohama. He put them all in a hotel room for ten straight days, working on the two problems: how to reduce the size and how to develop a tape recorder that would sell within the given price range. Day after day they worked, eliminating certain possibilities, developing others. At the end of that time they had conceived

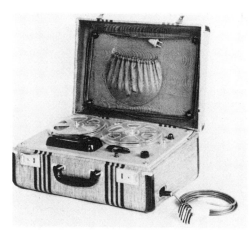

The improved H-1 tape recorder, first marketed in March 1951, and, obviously, portable.

a tape recorder that could be carried around like a suitcase; they had been unable to meet the designated price range but had succeeded in reducing the cost from 160,000 to 80,000 yen, halving the original price. This was the H-type tape recorder, developed in 1951.

With sixty or seventy tape recorders already sold, and the product beginning to attract attention, Kurahashi thought that Yagumo Sangyo should become its sole national agent. But top management at that firm thought this would entail too great a risk. When Kurahashi told Tokyo Telecommunications his disappointment, Morita said—with what was becoming for him a speed of decision-making unheard of among Japanese executives—"Then you join us. I'll set you up in a separate sales organization." Kurahashi promptly accepted, and at once found himself the head of the Tokyo Recording Company, a subsidiary with no staff and three directors. Tokyo Telecommunications had only about a hundred people at that time, and most of them were required for engineering and production. Only Morita and, soon afterward, one assistant, were available to work with Kurahashi.

They knew that Nippon Gakki Instruments, which marketed under the name of Yamaha, had an excellent pipeline into schools for pianos and other musical instruments, so they went to them and asked if they would put the tape recorder into their line. Though Yamaha then had a policy of only selling their own manufactured instruments, the president immediately saw the importance of the tape recorder and agreed.

But though Yamaha had a good network and knew how to sell musical instruments, they had no knowledge of electronics or electrical engineering; they could not answer the questions about the machine comfortably and thus could not sell it; when they did, they could not service it properly.

Morita became intimately involved with sales. He tried everything. He would get himself invited to a party, and appear with a tape recorder. Then he would play music or tape guests' voices all evening, and everyone would laugh and sing into the microphone and say what an ingenious machine this was. But at the end of the party there would be no sale—and the host would merely thank him for providing the entertainment. Morita began to wonder whether he was an inventor or an entertainer. "It's a very interesting concoction," they'd say, "but too expensive for a fancy toy."

Though he was the son of a sake brewer, Morita disliked drinking intensely; but liquor was still scarce then and the purchasing agents he dealt with wanted nothing more. Morita drank. He would take various agents to places he knew on the Ginza night after night. "It took lots of time and lots of drinking to promote a good relationship with them," he says ruefully, "but periodically there would be a change in the firm and I would have to start drinking with another purchasing agent." Yamaha continued to disappoint him with its sales performance. He was dependent upon that one purchasing agent for his principal sales, and the sales were not forthcoming. "This is deadlock," he thought. "This man is my only customer. If we come out with a new product someday and he says 'No,' that's the end of the story."

So Morita and Kurahashi began to go around to the schools themselves, in a Datsun truck they had recently bought, and while they did, Morita codified the central principles of marketing that his firm has essentially followed to this day.

With a new product you must educate your market first. They would sponsor meetings with schoolteachers and Morita would tell those gathered how the machine worked and how it could be used to record NHK programs, for use whenever they were most applicable; how they could record the voice and teach correct speech; how it could be used in social science education.

Never shy, Morita now showed an immediate genius for such selling. His vibrant voice became convincing, enthusiastic; he found dozens of uses for the tape recorder in the classroom. As a physicist and someone who had actually helped to produce the tape itself, he had an incisive grasp of all the instrument's technology. He had a natural flair for the dramatic, and lit the imaginations of the gathered teachers. In those classrooms and auditoriums Morita learned through the physical act the absolute necessity to communicate the usefulness of a given new product before you can expect any demand for it to exist.

The tape recorders began to sell.

"Education is communication," he said. "We must transfer our knowledge and information to as many people as possible."

Meanwhile, another issue emerged. Minnesota Mining's tape began to come into Japan. When England and Germany began to manufacture magnetic tape for consumer use, they were able to protect their industry by stopping all importation of tape. But in Japan, most commercial broadcasting stations, which were owned by or had the backing of powerful newspapers, began to bring 3M tape into the country. This became an important source of revenue for the Federation of Commercial Broadcasters, and Tokyo Telecommunications could do nothing to stop this severe competition. They had to compete on quality, always, with the excellent 3M tape, and were forced to press for greater and greater improvements. But whenever they advanced, 3M went even further.

In time, as Tokyo Telecommunications expanded their sales and improved their product, 3M came to realize the market force of this new little company and sent representatives to offer a joint-venture agreement. "They had excellent technology and very important patents that would have helped us immensely then," Ibuka recalls; "we were dying to get these." But 3M laid one important condition onto their offer: Tokyo Telecommunications would have to stop manufacturing tape recorders.

Though Ibuka sorely wanted the use of those patents and 3M's vast technological expertise, his tape recorder business was actually much larger than that for the tape. He could not afford to give it up—and neither he nor Morita wanted such outside control over what they could and could not produce.

The decision not to accept 3M's offer was extremely wise.

It clarified their determination to develop all the technology and all products by themselves. They would produce their own tape for their own tape recorders with their own magnetic heads.

"Much later," Ibuka told me, "IBM purchased tape-coating machines from us and other equipment for the manufacture of their own tape for their computers. Until then, they had been one of 3M's important customers. With IBM using our technology, we felt a distinct sense of triumph."

With Yamaha unable to do an adequate job, Morita determined that he must build his own distribution system. He had learned the value of communication and realized that the closer he was able to position himself with respect to the consumer himself, the less dilution of the education and the better his contact would be. If there had to be a "relay system" between the manufacturer and the consumer, he wanted to eliminate as many intermediary way stations as possible—so that the "education" and information that proceeded from him and Tokyo Telecommunications would not be distorted. Others in the firm were skeptical. They had no marketing staff of their own: It would take years before they could market their products directly. Couldn't the money and effort be expended better on research and development, on improving their plant and expanding their production?

"We must do our own business in the field," Morita insisted. "That way our effort can be accumulated. We can build a reputation and this will become a company asset. We *must* accept the expense and the difficulty now, in order to eliminate our dependency upon purchasing agents who might not be able to sell or service our products—or might not want to."

There were grave problems.

The expense of establishing such a distribution system would be immense. His customers would now be unspecified people rather than a handful of purchasing agents. Where would he find them? How would he reach them with his

A family photograph, 1951–483 employees. Ibuka is in the front row center, Morita is to his right, Higuchi is to Morita's right, and Iwama is directly behind Morita.

message? Could Tokyo Telecommunications service the products after they were sold?

No matter what problems arose, they *had* to establish their own channels. No matter how long this took. "Ten years from now," Morita said, "we should have our organization. We must be patient and put in the seeds." He would repeat this ten-year concept many times, with other products, in the ensuing years.

Morita began by getting two other companies to join together under his aegis and form another network to compete with Yamaha; they eventually became Sony Sales, the heart of Sony's highly effective distribution system in Japan today. Though competing networks produced good results at first, overcompetitive price-cutting began to occur, with the resulting threat that the entire price structure of the market would be destroyed. Within a half dozen years, the contract with Yamaha was fully terminated, and Tokyo Telecommunications had full control of its own distribution system.

Later, they learned another marketing lesson: Sales must be drawn from as wide an area as possible. In Kyushu, where they had enjoyed good sales for their tape recorders at first, the coal mines began to fold; sales soon dried up and they had difficulty collecting bills. They could never again depend on one locale, and knew that they would eventually have to become worldwide in their operations.

The basic work of educating the market showed positive results; the tape recorders began to sell extremely well. Within a year or two after Morita and Kurahashi began to visit schools throughout the country, about 30 percent of all elementary and junior high schools in Japan owned a Tokyo Telecommunications tape recorder, and the number continued to increase, with solid sales coming first slowly, then in a rush, from private consumers, banks, offices, the police, the entire broadcasting network (where many local radio stations actually started their operation through use of the tape recorder), and the

Schoolchildren gather around one of the first Sony tape recorders used in Japanese classrooms.

universities. Eventually, two-thirds of Japan's 40,000 schools bought the Tape-corder.

Within a few years of intensive work, the tiny Tokyo Telecommunications had pioneered its first new consumer product and established a firm financial foundation. Pioneering was beginning to pay.

CHAPTER THREE

Small Is More

Any invention or discovery is a great thing but to put it to practical use is even more important.

—MASARU IBUKA

TODAY SONY'S huge plant in Atsugi, about thirty-five miles southwest of Tokyo, boasts some of the most advanced and sophisticated facilities in the world for the development and mass production of semiconductor devices, ranging from silicon transistors and diodes to integrated circuits. More than two thousand carefully trained technicians help produce the transistors, and more than 150 engineers work constantly on the development of new systems. Rows of white-coated young women search patiently into high-power microscopes in the laboratory-like surroundings. Silicon crystals, weighing twelve to thirteen kilograms each, are produced in an automatic growing process that takes about fifteen hours; laser beams are used

A Sony semiconductor production line today.

to slice the crystal wafers, which are then polished and cut into pellets. One hears the methodical clicking of a delicate pellet-alignment controller as it pecks its way across the crystal slice, guided by a light sensor, picking up the tiny pellets by suction and placing them on a tray. In fifteen discrete processes, in dust and lint free rooms, the creation of the miniature transistors continues—the photoetching, the diffusion of impurities onto the pellet, the bonding of twenty-four gold lead wires onto integrated circuits.

To the layman it is a world of high mystery—a highly developed world in which science and practical wisdom have created a methodology for making hundreds of thousands of these powerful mini-devices each year. The transistor itself, invented in December 1947, is an electronic amplifying device utilizing the properties of single-crystal semiconductors (so called because they are *intermediate* in electrical circuitry between metals and insulators).

Dr. Makoto Kikuchi, director of the Sony Research Center and for many years a leading expert in the semiconductor field, says that the technology is highly matured now, that there will be fewer dramatic breakthroughs.

The device revolutionized electronics, and its advancement was exceptionally rapid and far-reaching in the 1950s and 1960s. Sony contributed its share: It has a long history of firsts in this field, which include the discovery and clarification of the tunneling effect by Dr. Leo Esaki in 1957, an event that led to his sharing the Nobel Prize in Physics in 1973.

A little more than twenty years ago, Tokyo Telecommunications knew nothing about transistors. Few people anywhere did. They had produced and begun to market an acceptable tape recorder, and with the growth of sales in the educational field, Ibuka decided to go to the United States for the first time and explore further uses that the tape recorder might have in schools. He had heard of the transistor, which had first been developed in Bell Laboratories, but until he went to America for three months in 1952, after Japan had been granted official sovereignty, he had scarcely thought that it would be of any interest to his company.

Ibuka visited the Pentagon, George Washington University, and the offices of many leading educators, and learned that, unlike in Japan, the tape recorder was being used to advantage in a large number of universities but very few elementary schools. His interest in science education, in particular, was whetted on this trip, and led to an abiding interest: He would soon help to establish the Sony Science Education and Promotion Fund to encourage scientific education throughout Japan and make the Japanese more science-conscious.

Toward the end of his visit, while staying in a noisy hotel on Broadway, near the old Roxy Theatre in New York, he learned something of great interest. Shido Yamada, a Japanese friend who had lived in America for many years, informed him that Western Electric had announced that they were going to start releasing the transistor patent. Yamada was to prove an invaluable ally over the next few years. Ibuka spoke English only slightly, and Morita not much better then, having learned from a non-English-speaking teacher in high school. Yamada, who had been doing stock-brokerage work, would become their first go-between, and they would never forget his help, freely given to the fledgling company. Yamada secured a copy of the draft offer from Western Electric but there was not enough time to arrange a meeting with the manager in charge of transistor devices before Ibuka was scheduled to return to Japan. Ibuka got the impression from the offer that an outright payment of $25,000 was required, not deductible from subsequent royalties, and this did not seem feasible: That was simply too much money for Tokyo Telecommunications at that time. But he left Yamada instructions to follow through, to see the people at Western Electric; the transistor was too intriguing to ignore.

Though Ibuka felt that the transistor would become an epoch-making device far in the future, he at first saw few prospects in it for his firm: The company was simply too deeply committed to the tape recorder, which was just beginning to sell quite well. But, curiously, because they were so interested in advancing their tape technology, they had recently hired a very large number of specialists in the fields of physics, applied chemistry, metallurgy, electronics, mechanical engineering, and related disciplines. Of their small staff, Ibuka estimates that about one-third were college graduates. Such highly qualified employees were a "source of considerable worry" to him, and as he returned to Tokyo he thought of some specific project that might occupy these experts, make them more productive, and keep them interested. He did not want them to grow bored; he did not want to lose any of them. He wanted them to feel that they had, at Tokyo Telecommunications, a chance to use their strongest scientific abilities.

Was the tape recorder enough?

Surely there was still important work to be done to improve that product.

Perhaps the transistor would provide the proper challenge, he thought. It would be difficult but it might mobilize them, draw forth their best efforts.

By the time he had arrived back in Tokyo, an idea began to crystallize. Higuchi remembers Ibuka saying, soon after he came back: "Radios. We're going to use this transistor to make radios—small enough so each individual will be able to carry them around for his own use, with power that will enable civilization to reach even those areas that have no electric power yet."

Morita, Higuchi, and other top managers were highly stimulated. In addition, Ibuka quickly learned that he had been mistaken about the payment; the $25,000 was not an *outright* payment but only an advance against patent royalties. There was a decisive difference.

Meanwhile, Yamada had talked to the Western Electric manager and described Tokyo Telecommunications and how it had developed the tape recorder in Japan all by itself. The manager was impressed. He wrote at once to Ibuka, expressing his admiration for the little company—and saying he would be pleased to license the patent to them; in fact, he urged them to sign an agreement as soon as possible.

Ibuka's great enthusiasm for the new, the untried, began to affect them all. Morita has told me: "I always trusted him absolutely—even when there was little more than a dream to build on. He has a great genius for innovation."

The $25,000, outright or against royalties, was a great sum for the firm, and the mere thought of applying this new technology to the production of portable radios seemed farfetched. They estimated that a single transistor device would cost from $10 to $50, and they knew of no one who had applied the device to radios. It is, of course, easy, once a transistor radio has been developed, once you know it can be done, to commit your resources to such a project; but the barrier of the unknown, whether it is for a sub-four-minute mile or some new electronics device, is awesome. Can the thing be done? How long will it take to get it done? Will it be worth the effort? Once it has been accomplished, by anyone, there is the comfort of the *known*. Probably no one else in Japan was then thinking about producing small transistor radios, inexpensive enough for anyone to buy. It was a tremendous risk.

One staff member immensely fired by Ibuka's enthusiasm was Kazuo Iwama, a young geophysicist who had left a volcanic rubble site to join Tokyo Telecommunications in June 1946, three weeks after it was incorporated. A measured, impeccably dressed, aristocratic man now, with a light laugh and an incisive intelligence, he says: "I had no knowledge of semiconductor devices whatsoever, but volunteered to head up a task force to study the transistor. I was very, very young." He was then in charge of tape recorder production but was relieved of this and all other duties to devote himself fully to this study of a subject about which he knew nothing, for which—as a geophysicist—he was not trained.

MITI, the government's Ministry of International Trade and Industry, was the competent authority in charge of overseeing all foreign contracts. Tokyo Telecommunications immediately applied for permission to sign a contract with Western Electric. In 1953 Morita went to America and signed a provisional agreement with them, contingent upon MITI's approval. While there, he secured every possible piece of reference material on transistors, including a massive two-volume "bible" called *Transistor Technology*. Iwama received this in August and at once formed a select team of four—a physicist, an electrical engineer, a chemist, and a mechanical engineer. They began to study *Transistor Technology*, which scarcely sounds like a bedside reader, intensely, discussing it and other semiconductor literature daily for four months. Being scientists they could understand the *science* of transistors well enough, but the technology was at first unintelligible; it was entirely new—they could barely visualize it.

MITI lingered. They would not commit their approval.

Foreign currency was so scarce in 1953 that there were sharp restrictions on all dollars payable abroad. MITI had to approve the contract before the finance minister would release the dollars for Tokyo Telecommunications to pay the $25,000 advance and seal the contract with Western Electric. They thought of Tokyo Telecommunications as a tiny outfit with a fine reputation for producing tape recorders and replacing communications equipment, but one that could not conceivably have the capacity to enter such a new and complex field as transistor technology. Why hadn't Hitachi, Nippon Electric, Matsushita, or any of the other huge electronics companies asked for permission to obtain a license for this new invention? If *they* weren't interested, why should MITI give Tokyo Telecommunications such a large allocation?

Ibuka, full of confidence, took the signed provisional contract with Western Electric to MITI to show them that since such a prominent American company recognized their ability to produce the transistor, why shouldn't they? MITI was not persuaded. In fact, they were furious. How could Tokyo Telecommunications have signed *any* agreement, provisional or otherwise, without their approval?

While MITI fussed over details, sending its experts to the firm's factory to look over facilities, Iwama and his team, relieved of all other responsibilities, continued with greater and greater intensity to study the texts Morita had brought back.

Finally, in January 1954, persuaded only by Ibuka's enthusiasm, MITI approved the contract, the advance was paid, and Tokyo Telecommunications had the right to use the transistor patent.

Most Japanese firms move with impeccable slowness, discussing a major commitment in the complicated *ringi*, or consensus, process of decision-making for months, even years.

Harvey Schein, now president of the Sony Corporation of America, remembers with dismay his first contacts, as a CBS group president, with Japanese firms. Discussions concerning a joint venture to distribute CBS records in Japan continued for well over a year, and still no decision was forthcoming. Finally, unwilling to wait longer, he drew up a list of possible other companies, someone agreed to introduce him to Morita, and the two had lunch. Schein says: "At that first lunch, we had a virtual agreement by the time we had gotten to the soup."

From the beginning the company was uniquely capable of moving with such speed. They were young and small and flexible. They owed nothing to tradition. Unlike most Japanese firms, they relied as little as possible upon the government or the banks. They valued and were capable of going their own way, at their own pace. Especially in the early years, their quick judgments were not always the best; Morita himself admits that he made many mistakes—snap judgments that sometimes took years to undo. It was the price of risk.

By mid-January 1954, only weeks after MITI approved the Western Electric contract, Ibuka and Iwama were on their way to America. Tape recorder sales were increasing daily; that would have to support them while they pursued the highly critical transistor project.

Western Electric was delighted that the little firm was able to act on the provisional contract. But the manager asked, for the first time, "What do you intend to use transistors for?"

Ibuka answered, "For radios."

The manager prudently pointed out how poor the yield was on the higher frequencies. About a dozen American licensees had been trying to make high-frequency transistors suitable for radios but none had yet succeeded in producing a commercially viable unit. He had assumed that, since they were essentially an audio firm, they wanted them for hearing aids. It was a logical assumption.

Ibuka knew that the yield on the lower frequencies was already satisfactory for mass production, and that Raytheon, producing for Zenith, was manufacturing thousands of junction transistors for audio use; these were mainly for hearing aids that used three transistors and sold for $150 to $500. He also knew that eyeglasses might be common in Japan but that Japanese were not in the habit of using hearing aids. Anyway, he was committed to the radio now. He *knew* it could be done.

During the next three months, Ibuka and Iwama were whirlwinds of activity. During the day they visited factories, plants, production facilities of all kinds, laboratories; Western Electric was exceptionally helpful. They went to Bell, where the transistor had been developed; to Westinghouse, to see a high-frequency generator; out to the Midwest, where a heavy-duty furnace was being used. They asked a thousand questions. Yes, the atomic purity of the crucibles had to be exceedingly high—but precisely what kind of crucible was Union Carbide producing? What kinds of oscillators were required to create the necessary heat? Could they acquire or make the necessary jigs?

And every night Iwama would write a long letter on what he had seen or learned—often as long as seven or eight neatly scripted pages on airmail foolscap. In Tokyo his four-man task force pounced on each report they got and began to order equipment based on the details and instructions they received. Some of the materials were available in Japan, few could be imported from America, some they prepared to create themselves. Telegrams sped the need to Tokyo.

NEED HEAVY DUTY DIFFUSION FURNACE. STOP

Then a telegram from Ibuka would arrive:

WAIT ON BUYING ALL EQUIPMENT UNTIL

FURTHER NOTICE STOP DETAILS IN A LETTER

Then more letters—letters filled to the edges with diagrams and instructions, Japanese interspersed with the English they were just learning for terms and processes entirely new to them.

In three months, by April, when Iwama and Ibuka re-

i) Zone leveling single crystal.

ii) boat ... ... quartz boat ...
(... single crystal ... Ge ...
... misorientation ...
quartz ...) ... Quartz ...
... pure ... paraffin wax ... graphite
... deposit ...

N₂ retainer Oval coil   graphite ring   N₂ Inlet
Out let

Quartz tube   Quartz tube   Quartz tube

... Silicon rubber ... Neoprane rubber ... no Sulfer ...
pulling Quartz tube ...
N₂ tube ...

... loose ... packing ... (detexile paper ... no Sulfer)

iii) N₂ の Inlet. Outlet ...
(Inlet ... Outlet ...)
流圭 ... 20 cub Cubic feet / hour ...

iv) ... Seed ... (2,2,1) ... Dimension
... ⅞" × ⅞" × 1½" ... この Seed ...
... retainer ... graphite retainer ...

v) coil. ring. interface ...

vi) ... Slider ... Quartz tube ... 3本 ...

vii) ... 装置 ... zone purification ...

A letter sent by Iwama from the United States on March 7, 1954, concerning the production techniques for transistors. This is merely one page from four volumes of such letters, most of which contain drawings, English phrases (where no Japanese equivalent yet existed), and highly detailed instructions.

turned to Japan, there were four fat folders filled with letters. I have seen them; they are a remarkable testament to foresight and tenacity. And they proved invaluable. By June, working with great intensity and speed, the company produced its first transistor device.

They had no way of knowing whether it would work until someone produced a Raytheon transistor voltmeter. Carefully they disengaged the Raytheon transistor device and put their device in that circuit. It worked. They had succeeded in making a successful transistor.

Then all that year they struggled to produce a transistor that would operate at sufficiently high frequencies for use with a radio. Periodically, as more and more personnel, time, and money were committed to the project, they feared they were endangering the financial stability of their little company. The market for tape recorders held and expanded; this alone supplied the capital needed to keep them going. By late 1954 they had indeed produced a transistor that could operate at high frequencies, but the yield was only about 5 percent, too small, they thought, for commercial production yet.

Then they received a final spur to their efforts. It is reported that one of those interested in the early 1950s in the Western Electric transistor patent was Texas Instruments, represented by two lean men in blue jeans and Stetson hats, who slouched down in chairs and, without much ado, leased the patent. They later produced the world's first transistorized radio for a company called Regency.

Ibuka and Morita now knew that they must go with what they had. It was time to pull out all the stops.

Early in 1955 they began to work out the complicated production techniques, all as new to them as the basic technology had been, and in August of that year they put the first transistor radio produced in Japan on display. Ibuka was radiant. Sen Nishiyama, who worked for the American Embassy then, remembers meeting him on the street and having him announce, full of unbounded smiles, "We've done it! We've made a transistor radio."

While they were working on the project, having more and more contact with the West, they decided they would need a a more suitable brand name. Tokyo Tsushin Kogyo Kabushiki Kaisha was a *bit* too cumbersome; few Americans could even pronounce it properly. "And any foreigner who cannot pronounce the name of a company," Morita thought, "is not likely to place much confidence in either its product or the company itself." They thought of using TTK, which was brief and easy enough, but there was already a TKK (Tokyo Kyuko K. K., Tokyo Express Company). They had used Tape-corder for their tape recorder and "Soni" (from "sonic") for its tape.

This was an important decision and they debated it for days. The new brand name would be used on the transistor radio, which they hoped to sell throughout the world.

If a Ford and a Chrysler were driven down the street, Morita reasoned, and you got only a quick glance at the name of both, you would remember Ford: It was shorter. They decided that the name should be composed of as few letters as possible.

And when it was spelled out, it should be easy to pronounce in Japanese as well as most foreign languages—and sound the same.

"Soni" was proposed—but this would be "so-naye" in English. But the base "son" from the Latin "sonus" (for sound) was good, and "sonny" suggested a mischievous little boy. Well, "We were a couple of sonny boys," Morita recalls—still young, still maverick. They almost chose Sonny, but Japanese would pronounce this as "Son-ny," which could be associated with the Japanese word "son," meaning "loss"—as in profit and loss. Not a happy idea. Finally they hit on Sony—which became the brand name for the transistor radio and then, in January 1957, the firm name.

They also considered the use of a logo, and actually as-

Japan's first transistor radio, the TR-55, marketed in August 1955.

signed their best designers the task of developing a distinctive sophisticated emblem. Several radios were eventually marketed with this, but their final decision was to drop the idea: It would take too much money to get people to memorize the mark. "Sony" would have to do the job, and the ad budget could be spent more effectively showing the *uses* of the products. Beyond that, Morita came to see that "the best way to sell products to invisible and unspecific great masses of people must be the establishment of an excellent reputation and confidence in our products—good products, good afterservice." Not lower prices or a fancy logo.

Soon all the major electronics companies in Japan were doing research in transistor technology, and Sony realized it would have to recruit as many new and able scientists in the field as possible if it was to maintain its hard-won edge. Iwama, attending a highly advanced diffusion symposium sponsored by Bell Laboratories, recognized with what rapidity the technology itself was advancing. They had mastered the basics, but that was only the beginning. "We'd had no idea," he recalls, "what we were in for. Now it was a race—and we decided when I returned from that symposium that we had to recruit the very best people."

Sony could not afford the luxury of traditional Japanese business ethics. It was still less than a decade old, and was beginning to grow at alarming speed. It needed new blood—experienced, well-trained scientists in the forefront of their field, managers of all kinds. At another symposium a short while later, Iwama heard a young man named Esaki deliver a paper, and he was so impressed that he promptly invited him to speak with Ibuka; the two of them persuaded Esaki to join Sony.

Other vital, shrewdly selected recruits followed—and it is because of Morita's and Ibuka's keen capacity to see in people what even they had not yet seen in themselves that the choices proved highly successful.

Over the next twenty years they acquired dozens of invaluable staff members at the higher levels.

They invited Noboru Yoshii, a forty-seven-year-old friend from the Mitsui Bank, to play golf with them one January afternoon—and on the way, Yoshii between them in the car, persuaded him to join the team; he is now senior adviser for financial affairs and has arranged Sony's listings on all the world's major stock exchanges.

When Kurahashi had demonstrated the tape recorder on the campus of Toyko University of Arts in the early fifties, he had been badgered by a young "very noisy" music student who kept asking all sorts of technical questions about this new invention, its possibilities, its flaws. Kurahashi didn't understand the technology himself so he put the man on the Datsun truck and drove him to headquarters. Ibuka and Morita were both highly impressed by Norio Ohga. When he graduated in 1953, they made him a special consultant; some years later, after he had launched a promising career as an opera baritone, Morita persuaded him to join the firm. Ohga was put—with no previous technical or business training—in charge of the tape recorder plant; he later became one of Sony's best negotiators in multimillion-dollar international negotiations. Ohga is now deputy president.

Dr. Kikuchi came after twenty-six years at MITI to head Sony's research center; he had hoped, after he retired from government service, to take a trip around the world but Ibuka called him at midnight and convinced him otherwise. A bright young man named Hajime Unoki, who speaks English with machine-gun rapidity, came from the petroleum industry and now heads Sony's international division; his father had answered a Sony ad on his behalf and he, thinking his father's urgent call meant that perhaps a meeting with a young woman had been arranged, came to Tokyo—where Morita insisted he join Sony. Shokichi Suzuki came from an import-export firm, went to America, he says, as Morita's "bag carrier," and was almost immediately made executive vice-president of the new Sony Corporation of America. An official from MITI came to inspect Sony when they had first petitioned for approval to sign the Western Electric contract; he joined Sony, served as general manager for the international division, and is now a senior managing director of Sony Sales. Shigeru Kobayashi was recruited from the printing industry, given charge of the Atsugi semiconductor plant, and told: "Do what you want." What he did has provided the backbone for Sony's unique plant-personnel policies.

One executive compared the company history, as seen in such appointments, to a "comic opera." But Morita and Ibuka chose well—then, with trust, gave these people a free hand. As one man told me: "I never worked so hard in my life. I never knew what hidden abilities were inside me until I came to Sony."

Sony set a goal of 10,000 transistors for its first year of production; it was only able to produce 8,000. (Iwama whimsically told me: "When there are enough, the market is saturated. The success of Sony is that we produce a little less than is required.") The number depended, monthly, on the percentage yield—how well the large single crystal could be made, how effective the slicing process worked, the emitter-collector relationship, their skill at etching the crystal. Since such technology had never been attempted before, it was a daily challenge. They tried one improvement, then another; if an improvement in the etching process suddenly increased the yield, the radio people rapidly pounced on the extra transistors.

So swift was the growth of Sony during the mid-fifties that structures or equipment were often obsolete by the time they were completed. They began to build a three-story ferro-concrete building near the main headquarters to house both a tape recorder and radio plant; both plants were barely housed there three months before more space was needed for transistor production, and tape production was forced out. A few years later this building became too small and they built the Atsugi plant.

The first transistor radio Sony produced was rather large. But Ibuka felt that since the small transistor device was being used instead of the vacuum tube, all else should be miniaturized too—the capacitor, the loudspeaker, the inductor, the transformer, even the batteries. He wanted a radio so small it would fit into a shirt pocket.

This presented grave problems, since most of the components for the radio were produced by subcontractors who at first refused to change their standard size. Ibuka asked the speaker manufacturer, and was told: A small speaker could not possibly be efficient; the sound would be poor and this would reflect on his reputation. They would not make such a product for Sony.

Until then, most Japanese manufacturers produced capacitors, inductors, and other radio components that copied both the design and size of similar products made in Europe and the United States. Ibuka disliked everything derivative—and needed a change if he was to produce what he now called a "pocketable" radio. Alone, he visited every component manufacturer Sony dealt with—arguing, beseeching them to take the kind of risks his company was willing to take. Sony couldn't produce the components themselves: They had to concentrate their resources on the transistors themselves, which no one could make for them. They *had* to get the cooperation of the component suppliers.

Finally they did. Ibuka single-handedly persuaded them.

And this brought about a major revolution in the Japanese component industry. The manufacturers could no longer rely on foreign models; they had to work out their own technology for miniaturization. It was a momentous change. Japanese manufacturers became independent of foreign technology—and Ibuka got his miniature radio, the Type 63, "pocketable."

Ibuka *(left)* and Morita, at a Sony plant, 1956. They frequently visit production facilities.

The world's first pocket-size all-transistor radio, marketed in Japan in March 1957.

Sony has continued to improve performance and reduce the size of its transistor radios. This is the world's first integrated circuit radio, the ICR-100, marketed in March 1967.

The TFM-151, Sony's first FM/AM transistor radio, marketed in America in April 1959.

Actually, the first models were slightly larger than a standard shirt pocket—so Sony made special shirts in which they would fit!

Sony sold over a half million of that one model, and a million and a half if similar models are included. Its sales soared. By 1955 Sony grossed $2½ million; between 1955 and 1957 it increased its employees from 400 to 1,200.

There was a gap of from two to three years before the major electronics companies could come out with competing —sometimes copied, under such names as "Somy" and "Sonny" —models, most produced through licensing agreements with RCA. By this time Sony had succeeded in increasing the cutoff frequency of transistors, getting them to operate at higher and higher frequencies.

They announced the first shortwave transistors in the world, and followed this with a transistorized FM receiver. A competing model did not appear for another four years.

CHAPTER FOUR

Scratching a Global Dream

*Products we design and manufacture should be sold
in the markets we develop following our own schedule.*

—AKIO MORITA

WHEN MORITA came to the United States for the first time
in 1953, primarily to sign the contract with Western
Electric, he received two shocks: American industry was posi-
tively awesome and the general American consumer still read
the phrase "Made in Japan" as infallible proof of cheapness.

"As early as the 1870s," suggests Noel F. Busch, "most
Japanese traders had concluded that their opposite numbers
from the United States and Europe were in most cases tasteless
bargain hunters interested in the cheapest merchandise available." So they made, chiefly for export, "Yokohama *muke*,"
which flooded the markets with jerry-built junk that became
synonymous with Japanese products. Only in 1950, when such

prominent photographers as Carl Mydans and Alfred Eisenstadt replaced their German Leicas with Japanese Nikons, did the West have a glimmer of Japanese technological skill. "The camera manufacturers," says Morita, "did us an invaluable service." But photography was a limited field—and what the best photographers knew of and used was not what the masses bought. It would take another decade or more for the association of Japan and junk to fade.

The United States, when Morita landed in San Francisco, seemed so huge, so advanced. "How can we compete with these people?" he wondered. He admits frankly that his first reaction was one of utter dejection: He felt defeated by the size and scale of American industry. It would be impossible to compete here, to sell his products in a country with such advanced technology, with such large, smoothly functioning companies.

After he had signed with Western Electric he flew to Germany; he was not more encouraged. Germany, too, had been destroyed in the war, but was already highly advanced. He visited Volkswagen, Mercedes-Benz, Telefunken, and other major firms—able to speak none of the European languages, bumbling and shy at first with his textbook high-school English. He saw virtually no other Japanese. English was the only foreign language he could manage at all, and he soon found himself relying on it more and more. "It was the only way to communicate," he recalls. "I knew it was the international language and that I would have to learn it." He carried a dictionary through Germany, France, and Switzerland, alone and often lonely or lost, making friends with an American who was also lost, finally growing bold with his English, recognizing that only when he lost all hesitation could he make the language the working tool it must become for him.

What he saw of European industry confirmed his feeling of defeat: He "lost all fight," he says; he could not possibly compete in this market either.

Only three years earlier, Edwin O. Reischauer had said: "The economic situation in Japan may be fundamentally so

Morita leaving on his first trip to the United States, 1953.

A rare photograph of Inagaki, Yamada, and Morita *(left to right)* in October 1953, eating a traditional Japanese meal at Yamada's apartment in New York City.

unsound that no policies, no matter how wise, can save her from slow economic starvation." Not only had the country been devastated but it was one of the poorest in natural resources in the world—needing to import more than 99 percent of all its crude oil, cotton and wool, and iron ore.

But despite the most dour predictions of wise observers, Japanese industry—and Morita's small company—had begun to grow. Steadily, through the marshaling of all its forces in what amounted to a national campaign, the little resource-poor country, defeated psychologically as well as physically by the war, was commencing what in less than ten years would be called "the economic miracle of Japan, Inc."

Morita does not like the phrase. To him it implies the total interdependence of government, industry, and Japanese people themselves in a coordinated effort. "Sony has grown," he insists, "solely in compliance with the principles of a free market economy, without much direct relationship to the government." But Sony was from the beginning a maverick—in Richard Halloran's fine observation, a *ronin,* or "masterless *samurai.*" With Honda and a very few other companies, it had gone and would continue to go its own way. Far more frequently than otherwise, Sony would actually pioneer management, financial, and marketing gestures that would seek to change the government's tight economic control.

Still, it is hard to conceive of Sony's growth without some understanding of how the entire country was beginning to lift itself, rung by rung, to economic prominence.

Reischauer, Halloran, Herman Kahn, Frank Gibney, William Forbis, and other shrewd observers have charted and detailed the reasons for Japan's remarkable growth—which saw the Gross National Product expand by more than 10 percent a year for more than two decades, industrial production *quadruple* in the decade from 1951 to 1961, and yearly per capita income rise from $17 in 1946 to $4,500 today, second only to the United States. Kahn isolates the following factors: an exceptionally high rate of personal saving (20 percent of disposable income); high technological capacity, supported by a severe nationwide commitment to higher education; strong personal motivation for economic achievement, backed by an almost Calvinistic work ethic and loyal, enthusiastic employees; excellent management of the economy by government, industry, and to some extent labor, with broad public commitment to economic growth and to surpassing the West. In addition, Japan had no defense budget; it had an almost inexhaustible supply of short-term money from the banks and firm government control of imports and investments by foreign industry; and there were less definable factors, like that curious equation of a firm's triumph with a national and personal triumph.

The roots of such growth were thus broadly set in Japanese character and an industrial ethic that had been emerging since 1868 when the Meiji rulers consciously began to seek an influx of the best Western ideas. Before the war the *zaibatsu*—vast financial cliques founded in the 1890s and including such giants as Mitsubishi, Mitsui, Sumitomo, and Yasuda—controlled 80 percent of the Japanese economy. After MacArthur's "Purge," which temporarily dismantled these joint-stockholding interlocking directorates, a new firm like Sony had a better chance to compete, but it still had to do so by developing new products and by pioneering new markets.

No matter where Morita traveled in Europe, attempting to find some promise of growth in the international market, he found no one who would pay any heed to the products of his little electronics company—and no evidence that he could market there.

Toward the end of his trip, Morita left Germany by train for Holland, to visit Philips, the huge electronics company. As soon as he crossed the border, everything changed. He saw the fields, farms, and windmills of a small agricultural country. People were riding bicycles, as in Japan. Philips itself impressed him tremendously—its size, its policies, the quality of its products, its worldwide sales power. But the effect this time was different. One man, born in a small town, had started an electrical business that grew to *this*—an international power. Perhaps Sony, still small and certainly still struggling, could rise, too.

From Holland, Morita wrote to Ibuka, telling him how encouraged he was by the sight of Philips. It *was* possible for Sony to become an international company; if they remained specialists, developed unique products within their own areas of expertise, continued and strengthened the policies they had already begun, they might even become "the strongest company in the world."

But they needed the proper product.

What they had achieved in tape recorder technology was impressive—but as yet essentially of local significance. Their tape recorder could not yet be the lever that would transform

Morita signing an agreement with a representative of Western Electric.

them from a small company, devoted to excellence, into a force in the international market.

Morita did not travel abroad in 1954; that was the year Iwama and Ibuka went to America to study transistor technology. But with his dream intact and beginning to take form, he went to America again in 1955 for three months.

This time he came with specific goals: He wanted to explore the market; he wanted to make concrete plans and preparations to distribute Sony products in America. He brought samples, but when he visited each of the hundreds of wholesalers and distributors his friend Yamada helped him locate, he told them he had not come to sell: He had come "to learn how to sell here."

He brought tape recorders, microphones, recording heads, and some specialized electronics equipment. He also brought a handmade test model of the still-unproduced transistor radio.

"This is the product," he had said when he saw how Iwama's research team was progressing. "This is the item that will launch us into the international market."

Morita returned to America in 1956; in fact, he began that year to make the trip a virtual commute, going two or three or more times a year, often for several months at a time. Today he has crossed the Pacific more than a hundred times and says: "It is a long commute." On this visit he began to seek actual sales, hoping to find enough companies who would import directly from Sony. He also met Adolph Gross, a manufacturer's agent in New York who treated him "like a son" and began to teach him the mechanics of American marketing.

The transistor radio was indeed of interest to American firms, and Morita began to make decent direct sales to many medium-sized retailers. Then he found one large company that wanted quotations for 5, 10, 50, and 100,000 transistor radios. Morita had not expected such large figures and told the purchasing agent he would have to let him know the next day.

A page of Sony products in the tenth anniversary catalog, 1956.   →

Testing before packing radios, 1956.

On a dynamic microphone production line, 1956.

When he returned, he said: "My company is a little bit different; our price goes down . . . then it goes up." And he gave the buyer the discounts he had established. The man was amazed to learn that though the discount grew larger from 5 to 10,000, after that it *diminished*. "I've been a purchasing agent with this company for thirty years," the man said incredulously, "and you are the first person to tell me the more we buy the *higher* the unit price will go!"

Morita explained that his company was small and needed protection. Certainly it would be good to get a big order; that's why he had come to America—to sell his products. But this was how he had analyzed the situation: A small or modest order would provide a sound addition to their production capabilities but for an order of 100,000 he would have to build a new factory, hire more employees, purchase more production equipment. If he didn't get a reorder the next year, where would he be? He would have an expensive new factory, and, since Japan had a lifetime employment system, he wouldn't be able to fire anyone. That order for 100,000 could bankrupt the firm! Unless he hedged. No, he would have to depreciate everything; the discount couldn't come down.

The buyer shook his head, laughed, examined the radio again—and settled for an order of 10,000.

Yamada also made an appointment with a prominent manufacturer on Long Island, whose brand name was one of the most respected in American industry. The purchasing agent was highly impressed with the radio and told Morita: "Yes, it's extremely interesting to us. We can move 100,000 through our network—but we will have to sell it under our brand name."

This was a big outright purchase by a well-established company with proven marketing skills. It could be a decisive sale for Sony and begin to earn back the enormous sums they had recently invested in transistor development.

But Morita balked. He would have to contact his people back in Tokyo.

For a week cables flew back and forth between Morita and the executive board in Tokyo. It sounded like an important order to the executive board, and they thought it might prove highly profitable—and lead to a valuable liaison.

No, Morita cabled, there are drawbacks.

True, they agreed—but can we live with them? Isn't there *some* way we can make this offer work?

Morita didn't think so.

They insisted: It really constitutes too large an order to turn down. "Get that order. Forget the Sony name."

In the taxi the next week, heading out past LaGuardia Airport to the company's executive offices, Morita told Yamada that Tokyo wanted him to accept the offer.

"Good!" said Yamada, smiling broadly.

"But I've decided to turn it down."

"No!" Yamada was shocked. He had lived in America for thirty years; the reputation of this company was unimpeachable. The power of their name was immense. Was Morita *sure* this was the proper decision? Was there no way he could change his mind? For an hour, talking rapidly in Japanese, they debated the issue. Yamada thought his friend was making a great mistake. This might be just the beginning; the company eventually might be able to market half a million transistor radios for Sony. More.

When they arrived, Morita told the buyer: "I regret, but we cannot take your order."

The buyer couldn't understand.

"I want to stay with the Sony name," Morita told him. "If you will use the Sony name on the radios, we will be willing to use your sales network, which I understand is excellent."

"No," the buyer said, starting to laugh. "Nobody in this country knows Sony; we couldn't sell *anything* under that name. But everyone in America knows *our* name. Isn't it ridiculous not to utilize our established reputation?"

"I cannot do it," Morita said.

"But we have a fifty-year history," the man said proudly. "Fifty years." He shook his head and smiled, astounded at Morita's innocence. "You have *no* history here."

Morita asked him: "Fifty years ago, how many people knew your name?" The man said nothing. "This is the first year of my company's fifty-year history," Morita continued. "If we don't use our name, we may not have a history."

Many other Japanese companies, faced with similar offers, accepted. Morita would not—and finally the American company did not take one radio.

Morita often calls this the single best business decision he ever made. Perhaps it was.

In 1957, convinced that he needed an American representative who fully understood the United States market, Morita contracted with Gross to have him serve as Sony's agent for five years, through his company, Agrod. In addition, an arrangement was made whereby a company called Delmonico International would serve as Sony's distributor.

Within a year Morita realized he had made a mistake. This was too similar to the Yamaha arrangement: He was locked in and would not have the direct control over marketing that had become so central to his sales concept in Japan. Dubious of Sony's ability to market by itself in a vast foreign country, he had signed away these rights and found that Delmonico was not nearly doing the job that he thought they should. They were interested in moving merchandise—not in product development, not in marketing or building a name. They paid little attention to the concept of after-sales service, which was becoming one of Sony's principal hallmarks. They didn't advertise to suit Morita's concept. Worse, they would take only sharply limited numbers of certain products, and refused at first to handle Sony's new AM/FM transistor radio—which Agrod had to bring in at its own risk; Agrod sold them out in four months. Still worse, Delmonico kept insisting that Morita produce a cheaper model radio, with six rather than eight transistors. Morita would not think of it.

Though he liked Gross, Morita realized that he should not have gone to an agent in the first place. He liked no part of the Delmonico arrangement and could see that it could cripple all his hopes.

Irving Sagor, who served as Gross's accountant at the time, says: "Morita knew this wasn't the kind of distribution he wanted and that the easiest thing was to roll over and play dead. Let them live out the contract and then rebuild." Instead, he decided to push ahead, do the job himself by advertising the products and the Sony name vigorously with money from Tokyo. He was taking the long view. Foremost in his mind was the establishment of Sony products and the Sony name in America. "He knew that his products were good and that there was a strong market for them here," says Sagor; "he had infinite patience." And even under the difficult circumstances, Sony's radio, at $39.95, was outselling $12 and $13 models; Sony was merely known in those days, says Sagor, "as the maker of the radio that works."

Then Gross died suddenly and Sagor, chiefly to help Gross's widow, took over control of Agrod.

There are astonishingly few lawyers in Japan—about 10,000 for a population of somewhat over 110 million; in America, for nearly twice Japan's population, there are roughly thirty times that number, some 300,000. Japanese draw up contracts more through a meeting of minds than written words. In his first Western contracts, Morita took the verbal understanding that had been reached between the parties to be the most important—if unwritten—clause. Litigation is not a prominent Japanese characteristic, and Morita had not been accustomed to reading contracts closely. As a result, when some agreements made in the late 1950s proved disappointing, he invariably lived by his word rather than looking for loopholes.

When Gross died, Morita says he began to look at the contracts closely. In doing so, he realized that the contract Sony had with Agrod had died with Gross. This would mean that Sony was now partially free of commitments that were hampering its growth in America. But Morita, without hesitation, decided to honor the contract. "I had given my word," Morita told me. "Adolph Gross had been my friend."

Sagor says: "Morita treated me as the incarnation of Adolph Gross."

Shokichi Suzuki, a tall, quiet man, joined Sony in March 1959. He had been Morita's classmate in high school and had been working for an import-export company when Morita approached him. Suzuki's bailiwicks had been India, Pakistan, and Hong Kong; Morita wanted him for Sony's burgeoning international division. As part of his initial sales pitch, Morita promised Suzuki's wife that if he went abroad it would be for definite short stays. This had been a problem for the Suzukis: Every time the man went overseas, he stayed an extra week or two. This would all be changed, Morita promised. "My company is different. If I say two weeks, I will send him back in two weeks."

In January 1960, Morita decided to take Suzuki with him to America so the man could see Sony's largest export market firsthand. So Suzuki came, he says, as Morita's "bag carrier, for two weeks."

"Is two weeks definitely the correct time?" he asked, so he could tell his wife.

"Yes, sure," Morita insisted; "absolutely no more."

Shortly after the two arrived in New York, relations with Delmonico exploded. The contract stipulated that Delmonico would handle Sony radios. But in late January Morita learned that they had advertised to the trade that they would be handling "the world's first transistorized TV"—a new Sony development that had been announced in Japan only a month earlier, in December, with indications that it would be marketed first in Japan, within six months. Delmonico had absolutely no authority to do this. Indeed, Morita had had no intention of allowing them to handle this new product; the contract specified radios, not television sets. But, without any agreement and certainly no knowledge of what the F.O.B.

prices would be, they even announced specific prices for the transistorized television. It was, on top of everything else, a fatal gesture.

Morita contacted Edward F. Rosiny, Gross's lawyer and a close friend of Sagor.

What could be done?

Rosiny began talks with Delmonico on February 1. The negotiations were tense—and complicated by the fact that the distributor had nearly a million dollars' worth of Sony radios. There were threats. If they couldn't handle the new television, they would . . .

Every night that week Morita called Japan, explaining how the situation had progressed, working out new plans. Delmonico was surely the wrong distributor and Sony had made a bad mistake; there was only one path Sony could follow and they should do so quickly—terminate their association.

Morita briefed Suzuki, who had been in America merely a few days now, on the Sony staff less than a year, and Suzuki agreed that they should try to terminate the contract if at all possible.

But what then?

Morita told him: "We will market by ourselves."

Suzuki was shocked. No Japanese company had yet tried to market their own products in America; all used agents or distributors.

"Is it possible?" he asked.

Morita shrugged and said: "I don't know. I don't know how it will turn out, or how we will be able to do this. But we must try. Otherwise, we will always be in a position where some distributor will be able to push us around."

"But if we can't?" asked Suzuki, who had no knowledge of the American market whatsoever. He knew *he* could not be of much help, and Morita would be needed back in Tokyo.

"If we fail," said Morita evenly, "we will still accumulate experience that will be an invaluable asset for the company."

What a wise, bold, and courageous attitude, Suzuki remembers thinking.

"We will be pioneers," said Morita, "the first Japanese manufacturer to go into the American market and distribute directly. And *you* must remain here as executive vice-president to run things."

Suzuki blanched.

By February 7 they had all agreed that this was what they would push for. Two days later, Sony headquarters in Japan had secured permission from the Japanese Ministry of Finance to establish a wholly owned subsidiary in New York, and a half million dollars of initial capital was established for the new company by Mitsui Bank of New York, Sony's principal banker.

Delmonico was now willing to discontinue the relationship—but they demanded $400,000 in compensation.

Such a figure was out of the question. It was unjustified by the circumstances—and it would cripple the new project, perhaps fatally.

Rosiny, Sony's new American lawyer, who would in later years prove to be a prodigious worker and an extraordinarily able negotiator—especially in licensing as well as other agreements entered into by Sony with Paramount, 3M, DuPont, Ampex, IBM, Tektronix, CBS, Union Carbide, and a host of others—decided to institute a lawsuit against Delmonico for appropriate redress on the theory that Delmonico had wrongfully misrepresented that it would be the distributor in the United States of Sony television sets; that its solicitation of dealers to handle the sale of such sets was totally unauthorized; and that its suggested dates of delivery as well as the selling price of such sets were wholly unfounded. All these acts allegedly impaired the reputation of Sony and should be enjoined.

In the days immediately following the inception of the lawsuit, discussions began with the object of terminating Delmonico's contract to distribute any Sony products. Delmonico's initial demand of $400,000 was unacceptable; in discussions with Rosiny, they reduced this to $300,000 and then to $200,000. Both Morita and Suzuki thought this was a victory and that they should accept. Rosiny insisted on going back to the negotiating table again and again, and finally settled for $75,000.

In another week they had completed negotiations for Delmonico's inventory of Sony products, inspected the radios, and raised an additional $500,000 from Mitsui.

Then, in mid-February, moving with lightning speed, Morita arranged to have all the radios—AM/FM, TR-610, 3-band, marine band—transported by truck from Delmonico's warehouse in Long Island City to 514 Broadway in New York City, where Agrod's office was located. Sagor, Suzuki, Morita, and a young man named Kazuya Miyatake (whom Sony had sent to Columbia University on a scholarship) began work at ten that morning. Each donned a uniform and helped to load and unload. It was a bitterly cold day but they could not afford to keep the truck overnight and decided they had better finish the entire job of bringing crate after crate no matter how long it took. They did not finish until three the following morning.

Exhausted, starved, they sat together in the old Agrod office on lower Broadway. Miyatake, who was in charge of counting the radios, decided to double-check his figures and left the office. Sagor automatically locked the door, activating the alarm system.

Then they took off their uniforms, drank some hot coffee, and began to talk about their plans. Agrod was the import agent and the new corporation would function as the distributor of those Sony products imported by Agrod. Morita said that they would make an announcement to the trade by February 20, saying that the Sony Corporation of America was officially in business and would start distribution on March 1. Morita, at least, was dauntless.

When Miyatake came back, he tripped the alarm system,

terrifying them all. Minutes later, security guards rushed in to find three weary Japanese and an American huddled around a desk in the old warehouse office.

What were they up to? It looked highly suspicious.

It took Sagor an hour to convince them, by producing his driver's license and some Agrod papers, that he was the president of Agrod, and that they should all be allowed to get some sleep.

They didn't get back to their hotel until five that morning.

Slightly more than a week later, the Sony Corporation of America opened for business—with three shabby desks, one telephone, three employees, a narrow, shoddy area in the back room behind Agrod's office, and a goal of 6,000 radio sales a month. Miyatake was pulled abruptly out of Columbia; calls to Tokyo brought several service engineers to New York within days—Morita already insisted on establishing service *before* sales; and Suzuki was told he would have to stay in New York for at least six months.

"My wife was furious," Suzuki recalls with a shake of his head and a broad smile. "I lost her trust completely."

Three months earlier, the Emperor's New Year's poem had proclaimed:

> *This is my wish:*
> That the rays of the rising sun
> May impartially light the corners of the world.

Sony had begun to bring at least sound.

On March 1 the one phone began to ring early, and didn't stop until that evening.

Morita had scratched a toehold in a new world.

CHAPTER FIVE

Amae and Jibun in Sony Plants

Structure follows strategy.

—PETER F. DRUCKER

Size separates.

If there are eight employees in a firm, the chief executive knows each of them intimately; he may sit at their workbench, share menial chores, know their families and their skills and their dreams; each worker may share responsibilities that span the lowest and highest kinds of work. When there are twenty or fifty, the links become more tenuous; at the bottom of the pyramid, you have unskilled or partially skilled workers; above them you must have supervisors or middle managers; top management is already several removes from the bottom and must assume its discrete responsibilities. At its worst, such expansion merely follows C. Northcote Parkinson's hilarious example of his law that "work expands so as to fill

the time available for its completion": Managers want to mul-
tiply subordinates; a civil servant hires seven officials to do
the work he once did alone.

Sony did not have to "make" work; its principal problem
soon became finding enough qualified people to fill the jobs
its dramatic increase in production and sales required. It grew
in fits. By the early 1950s it had 300 employees; by 1958, the
number had grown to 1,550; in 1961, the year of its fifteenth
anniversary, there were 4,405 employees—and the number
would continue to soar, to 15,081 by 1970 and 22,108 in 1975.

Such growth can be traumatic, disruptive; it can wrench
companies from their original management ideals. It creates
the need for personnel managers, supervisors, chains of command, pension plans, sophisticated budgeting systems.

In Japan all this is complicated by the unique Japanese
characteristic of *amae,* dependency. There is even a brilliant
book on the subject, *The Anatomy of Dependence,* by Dr.
Takeo Doi, a world-renowned Japanese psychiatrist. *Amae* is
the desire to be passively loved, with an attendant abandon-
ment of *jibun,* the self, to some larger group of which one is a
part—the family, the state, the corporation. It grows from the
traditional Japanese syndrome of preferring to be dependent
rather than independent, group-oriented rather than self-reliant,
conforming rather than innovative. *Amae* explains in part why
so many Japanese are, in Ruth Benedict's words, "terribly concerned about what other people will think of their behavior."

Amae begins in infancy and is fostered by the highly in-
tricate relationships one learns to have with those above and
below one in age and position; I suspect it is even encouraged
by the traditional bow, the sign of deference to another, and
the strong sense of *giri ninjo,* social duty and filial devotion.
Some observers have called *amae* "the cancer of the country,"
the fear of doing things alone, the will to lose oneself in one's
duty to a corporation. In industry the lifetime employment
system is perhaps its most visible emblem. An employee, says
Halloran, "pledges fealty to that organization in much the way

a *samurai* pledged his loyalty to his *daimyo*. In turn, the organization pledges its paternal obligations to the employee. He will not be fired except for criminal malfeasance or gross scandal."

"A Japanese company," says Morita, half-jokingly, "sometimes looks less like a business than a social-welfare organization."

But these characteristics—dependence and conformity—are alien to Sony's basic management concepts. From the start the firm had vowed to support independence and innovation, to unfold the self of each employee. The problem became, ironically, could Sony's principles survive their own success? Or would the growing company become just another large, traditional Japanese corporation—rigid and heavily paternalistic?

Sony met the needs of growth at the higher levels by breaking Japanese tradition—by which few people leave one firm in midcareer to join another—and winning away capable people from other companies; Morita openly uses the verb "steal." It had no alternative. It needed qualified people at once; it had no time to train them. The most severe problem was the increasing distance between top and bottom. Iwama, who had worked so hard on the development of the transistor and had then—as Morita began to explore the foreign market—become increasingly responsible for executive matters, says frankly: "The semiconductor factory, where the trouble started, had grown too quickly. Management was too busy with technology and marketing problems. Sometimes we forgot the problems of people. I myself didn't pay enough attention then to human relations with employees."

One of the upshots was the first (and only) strike in Sony's history. It evolved from the traditional "spring struggle" with labor in 1961, and culminated that May in an abrasive fifteenth anniversary strike.

Few strikes have simple causes. All represent a final breakdown of adequate communication. The strike at Sony was no exception. If the company had, in its rapid expansion, become remiss toward its workers, the union had become too pug-nacious.

The labor situation in Japan differs sharply from American practice. Though there are in some industries, such as electronics, loose federations of unions, these industry-wide groups are essentially forums; the significant bargaining force is the company union, organized by the individual plant and closely affiliated with all other plant unions in a given company. The unions and the company are traditionally close, and before 1961 Sony's labor relations were marked by mutual trust. The union slogan was: "To prosper with Sony." With the lifetime employment ethic at the heart of this relationship, workers and management are part of a fate-sharing pact: Management knows that all the time and effort and money it spends to train, educate, and care for its employees will be a sure company asset for years to come; the workers know that whatever efforts they devote to the company will increase its reputation, stability, and growth, and their security. In America unions are often only *against* something; here much of the actual detail work connected to personnel management was frequently handled by the Sony unions themselves. Sony management, acknowledging the mutual trust of such a relationship, had accepted a union-shop agreement.

Initial labor demands for the new year are presented in the late fall, then negotiated in what is commonly called the "spring struggle," or "spring offensive." These negotiations are rarely the mere formalities they are often called but they are, through the medium of the consensus method of reaching a decision, invariably resolved. Until the spring of 1961, Sony's spring struggles had been governed by exceptional good faith: The company was growing and it had a generally liberal appreciation of labor's role.

But that year, though the top federation leaders remained moderate, there was increasing influence from a left-wing element in the group that began to produce a harsh note in the relationship with Sony. The company was a plum. Its growth had been spectacular. A strike on its fifteenth anniversary, when the prime minister and other government dignitaries were scheduled to be on hand, would cause the company to lose face.

With mutual trust gone, Sony did not feel it could renew the union-shop agreement. Though the union's demands for 1961 did not warrant a strike, the *tone* of the negotiations was different this time. The relationship deteriorated all that winter; negotiations became more and more tense; eventually Sony agreed to a wage raise beyond which it simply could not go. The union became adamant. Some employees dropped out of the union, others formed another union of their own. Suddenly there were three different groups of employees.

The adversary union, strongly pressured by the left-wing element in the federation, had control of many of the young women, junior high school graduates, at the Atsugi semi-conductor plant—several hundred of them, many quite young and naïve—and scattered support throughout the company. Believing that their threat to embarrass Sony management on its anniversary would bring the company to its knees, the union keyed its strike threat to the celebrations planned for May. Management did not buckle; it could not afford to and it could not permit the precedent. In fact, it resolved at that time to separate specific management of the plants from labor-relations negotiations with the union; it established a strong labor-relations team, and a separation of functions that has persisted to this day.

Though the strike itself lasted no more than a total of five or six actual days, with intervals between them, it caused considerable mischief. Conditions at the Atsugi plant worsened daily throughout April; production schedules could not be met. Each day the union would bring to Sony headquarters busloads of Atsugi workers, reinforced by as many supporters from other unions as it could muster. Picket lines were established around the entire building to obstruct entry (though many employees broke through them to get to work), placards and red flags were raised high by the boisterous crowd, and

A quiet moment at the fifteenth anniversary strike.

mottoes were painted in bright bold letters on the walls. The most spectacular demonstration was on May 7, the actual day of the fifteenth anniversary.

And then it was over.

In the end, Sony management did not increase its wage offer by one penny: It merely changed the wording of the agreement to help the union save face. Within weeks, the Atsugi plant was functioning smoothly again.

Though Sony effectively separated labor relations from actual plant management, it recognized that the two are inter-dependent. Its founding spirit had included a promise to estab-lish "an ideal factory—free, dynamic, and pleasant," and Morita and Ibuka knew they must rededicate themselves to the task of doing just this. The engineers and research technicians had retained their vital enthusiasm, and if this had not fully filtered down to the blue-collar worker, they felt it their obligation to see that it did.

They had recently hired, as a part-time contract adviser, a warm, soft-spoken man, then forty-seven, by the name of Shigeru Kobayashi. He had been variously involved in labor relations and plant management in the printing and publishing industries but had no experience whatsoever with electronics. Ibuka called Kobayashi to his office and asked him if he would become plant manager at Atsugi. He agreed, but immediately said he ought at least to read some good books on transistor technology first; he knew nothing about it. "There's no need for such study," Ibuka told him. "You wouldn't understand the books even if you did read them." Then he said: "I shall not mind if this plant has to be shut down. I will take the responsibility for that. You are free to do there whatever you like. Try to do something truly creative."

I asked Ibuka about this gesture of his, and other similar gestures of his incredible trust. He said: "We must have fixed production and budgetary requirements, but within these limits we try to give Sony employees the freedom to do what they want. This way we draw on their deepest creative potentials. Kobayashi found a human connection to every employee in that plant."

Kobayashi was astounded at Ibuka's delegation of full free-dom. He had never heard a top-management official make such a statement—nor had he heard of one being made anywhere in Japan at the time. Ibuka's words gave him, he told me, "a remarkable sense of mission. I became fascinated, then intrigued by the challenge—the sense of the freedom and responsibility I was being given."

Kobayashi has written fully of his experiences at Atsugi in two books eventually printed as one and published in English as *Creative Management*. The book, which has sold nearly a quarter of a million copies in Japan, is a remarkably human document—sometimes (as he now admits) naïve, at times proving impractical, but always human. He clarified and expanded many of the issues when I talked with him for several hours in Tokyo.

He remembers that on the day he assumed authority at the plant, he stood before all the workers, most of them "irresistibly young," "cheerful, so smiling," and from his heart blurted out: "I don't know anything about transistors but I like human beings very much. Let's do our best together."

Kobayashi immediately isolated several important issues in plant management: Most workers had what he amusingly calls a "small-pebble complex" (fearing themselves insignificant), and most problems emerge from this and from lack of adequate communication.

He examined conditions carefully. Where had the original Sony spirit, to bring out the best in each person, gone awry? What could be done to restore a full measure of vitality?

Part of the problem, he saw, was that in growing so rapidly, "imitative, pseudo-scientific management" on the part of some overzealous managers—often influenced by Frederick Taylor's scientific time-and-motion methods—had resulted in *contrived* methods of increasing motivation and efficiency. These, in effect, began with the premise that people were "machines or domestic animals." A human factor was missing. Essential trust was missing in the personal relationship of management to the workers.

A labor regulation, for example, required that women workers be given one day free a month, during their period;

some managers demanded that women be sent to the clinic and actually inspected before they could receive an extra needed day. Kobayashi, horrified at this crude invasion of privacy, immediately revoked the inspections. A cafeteria problem emerged soon after he came: Service was so slow that many employees were losing most of their lunch break waiting on lines. There were two alternatives: enlarging the service counters (which could be done for a minimal sum) or increasing the number of attendants (which would be expensive). When Kobayashi proposed the former, and the elimination of *all* attendants—so that employees would have to be trusted to pay voluntarily for each meal by depositing their meal coupons in an appropriate box—many of his colleagues scoffed. They insisted that the company would not collect *one-third* of the required tickets. Kobayashi disagreed: Not only could the workers be trusted but *they would try to live up to the trust placed in them.*

Today, when the Atsugi plant has five times the number of employees it had then, this system is still in use, along with the brightened atmosphere Kobayashi inaugurated of small tables with flowers on them, instead of the long rows previously used. The employees themselves maintain a large graph that charts the honesty of their co-workers. It registered close to 100 percent when I was there, and had never dropped more than a few percentage points below that level.

The principle was an important one: If workers are treated merely as "tools of management," if they are treated inhumanly or without trust, they will revolt.

The key is trust. True trust. Not trust as a *tool* but as a living concept governing human relationships.

Power and authoritarianism can also become sharp impediments to a trusting relationship. Kobayashi had seen eager new workers—immature, unspoiled, but "admirably hopeful" —have their spirits broken by managers who merely wanted them "to do as they are told, obediently and without question." Hopeful expectations for a work career would be crushed quickly by "surveillance based on the carrot-and-stick philosophy, simple meaningless tasks endlessly repeated," and severe authority.

Was there no way to avoid this waste of human potential?

Many firms attempted to do so by coddling employees under the widespread paternalistic system used in most Japanese industries—providing extraordinary facilities and all-encompassing benefits, "buying" their labor with sweets or imposing such contrived gimmicks for motivating "love of company" as a daily company song or sermon. One rather infamous and often-quoted company song ends:

> *Grow, industry, grow, grow, grow!*
> *Harmony and sincerity!*
> *Matsushita Electric!*

There *is* an old Sony song, but when I asked plant managers about it, they said no one remembered the words; it had been composed and sung many years earlier by an employee choral group, not by the general plant workers.

Wasn't such paternalism essentially psychological manipulation? Didn't it have as its base a low view of people and a low view of work itself? Several of the most bitter strikes in industrial history had in fact been against the Hershey Chocolate Company in Pennsylvania and Pilkington Brothers Glass in England—both extravagantly paternalistic companies before then. And Krupp so overcommitted itself to such worker aid that, unable to maintain its benefits, it was brought to the brink of financial collapse.

Kobayashi found such methods degrading and ineffectual. Ultimately, the solution must lie in the *quality of the work experience,* in a trust that would allow workers to control their own personal and working lives more fully. In effect, he was proposing exactly the opposite of the paternalistic system: maximum freedom from any sort of company control. "All human beings," he says, "deep down, have the desire to devote themselves to work as the central element in their lives." If they can do this, and have control of their lives—which is the primary good in itself—then eventually they will take pride in their work, in themselves, and in their company, and will have *earned* such pride.

But how could this be brought about?

Kobayashi had begun in the purely personal realm—the cafeteria; he soon extended his concern to the dormitories in which many of the Atsugi workers lived. "The concrete buildings then provided by Sony were cold and unattractive," he recalls, "and so were the dormitory 'mothers.'" Employees with *real* homes could return to them and "revive their humanity." Dormitories should "not be just containers of workers for the benefit of the company," they should be as close to a real home as possible; the workers should control their own lives. So, in a bold step, he severed connections between the management of the dormitories and the plant organization; then he arranged for new dormitories to be constructed, and finally encouraged the building of small prefabricated homes where four to eight girls could do their own housekeeping. The latter—which were the first of their kind in Japan—are pleasant buildings today, with a common kitchen and dining room, and neat sleeping rooms individually decorated. The workers pay for their rooms, and learn to live with full autonomy. He encouraged a "coaching system," whereby one of the senior workers (rather than some plant representative) would live with five new recruits for three months, to help orient them to their new lives. There were no company-imposed rules but the residents themselves composed "A Guide to Dormitory Life for Health and Happiness."

Though there was a struggle to implement these innovations, along with the elimination of time clocks and the encouragement of autonomy in recreation (rather than the traditional hyped-up company teams), this began to erode much of the small-pebble complex. The workers were beginning to be responsible for the quality of their own lives, and Kobayashi says this immediately showed in their revived spirits.

Special housing units for female employees at Atsugi.

The nursery and kindergarten, which follows the Montessori method, at Atsugi.

In the work sphere he pressed for similarly personal solutions.

When he came to Atsugi, the fact that he knew no one in the factory and nothing about electronics required that he study the technology, talk constantly to the workers and engineers, watch and observe carefully. "Had I come as an expert in the management of an electronics plant, I would have made different decisions," he says. "But the physicial actions of learning afresh formed the basis of creative management."

When someone on the staff came in with a suggestion he had to approve, he was unable to make a decision until he knew what the suggestion meant. "I would ask all sorts of silly questions at first," he says, "and the man would have to teach me. At first he might look down on me and even speak condescendingly—which I didn't mind. But as I probed more deeply, asking more and more questions, I noticed that he was perhaps adjusting his original position. Sometimes I would ask unexpected questions, and the man would be challenged to explain the problem with greater clarity, which helped *him* understand it better. And when I had finally understood, and could see that the man was confident and reliable, I would often say I was leaving it all up to him. I would take the responsibility; he only had to do his best." It was the same challenge Ibuka had given Kobayashi—and the men, like him, gave extra effort to make their change work.

"Trust cannot be built upon fear that one's trust may be betrayed," says Kobayashi in *Creative Management*. "Trust can flourish only when one is willing to abandon oneself in the act of trusting. When a man who is truly willing to assume responsibility sincerely trusts his people, a corresponding sense of responsibility will be aroused in them. Courage and gentleness, therefore, are like the two sides of a shield."

Could these qualities be built into the structure of the plant itself? Kobayashi thought they could. With shrewd foresight, he began to develop systems of vertical and horizontal interconnecting teams or cells. Each was composed of from two to twenty members engaged in a specific plant process, each met once a week, and each was connected to all the others. The logic behind the system was to avoid the normal authoritarian chain of command, establish specialized units that could take charge of their own work, give each worker a more intimate connection to a work unit. As members of such a small group, the workers developed a team spirit and the capacity to buoy their team members, even compensate for the possible weakness of some, share valuable information, and establish team goals. The cell system thrived not on "command and orders but, rather, *information,*" which flowed into each cell from below, above, or from the sides. With the information—goals, facts, activities—the cell would meet, decide what methods to follow, what role was to be played by each member, and then begin their work. When the work was completed, the group reviewed its performance.

Sony Ichinomiya plant (color TV assembly).

Kobayashi also held a regular monthly meeting in which he spoke with the entire work force about production achievement and new goals, introduced new workers, praised superior performance. He was beginning to knit the plant together.

Sony management, particularly Ibuka—who had long been deeply interested in education—had already instituted unofficial high school courses for the benefit of the workers. "They are not being offered to you for the benefit of Sony or for the sake of molding people who will be compatible with Sony," Ibuka told the first students. "I only want you to study to be fine human beings." By 1963 Sony had put up 200 million yen toward having this loose program turned into a certified private high school, and a year later Sony Atsugi High School was formed, where, for 5,000 yen a month, students could study after hours. Though Sony had invested heavily in the program,

The Inazawa plant (color picture tubes).

The Osaki plant (color television) in Tokyo.

unlike education at other Japanese companies, it was supported mainly by tuitions from the workers. This required a much more serious approach on the workers' part; Kobayashi says he was "speechless with emotion" at the first commencement exercises, when he saw some of the first graduates who had repeated the first grade over and over in their determination to earn the coveted degree.

Kobayashi's concepts produced marked progress in the human realm. By avoiding a "welfare," or "paternalistic," approach—methods he strongly dislikes—and attempting to create a true community, uplifted by the best in each worker, he was discovering the true roots of motivation. Workers were becoming more attached to their work, more enthusiastic and discerning about their performances.

The results in business terms were impressive. Absentee-

A magnetic tape production line.

ism went down sharply, morale was high, production increased significantly.

It is now nearly ten years since Kobayashi retired from his post as plant manager of Atsugi. The plant has changed. The problem of size, which he foresaw as the most severe threat to the individual worker, is greater now, the links are looser. Even the type of worker has changed with the new generation; there are now eight hundred mostly urban housewives in the plant, where before most of the workers were young girls from farms. The plant now produces U-Matic video tape recorders and the Betamax unit as well as semiconductors. And what of the other twenty-odd plants in Japan, those producing color tubes or tape, audio equipment, television sets, digital time devices?

Some of Kobayashi's concepts have not weathered well.

"He tried to mix everyone together," one manager told me. "He insisted that everyone be allowed to participate in every meeting—highly sophisticated engineers, middle managers, and line workers, cleaning women and cooks. That could work when the plant was small and the technology less sophisticated. But top engineers would grow bored by the 'How to make soup' problem and line workers couldn't understand a word of high-level technical discussions. We experimented, but the method was too oversimplified for our present needs."

Though production technology for semiconductors—with its autonomous stages, each with its discrete policies and its own chief—differs totally from that of the production line that creates Trinitron tubes or assembles television sets, the challenge, in new and more difficult terms, still lives in all the plants: Find the most human way to encourage unity, teamwork, and creativity.

The specifics of Kobayashi's revolution in plant management may have changed but as I visited various divisions of the Atsugi plant, the picture-tube plant at Inazawa, and the television assembly lines at Ichinomiya, and spoke with the managers, I could see that his spirit was very much alive. The major emphasis is still on human values, human motivations. Each worker is still encouraged to find a true sense of attachment not only to his or her task but to the entire process; the cell system is still used and it still enables a worker to avoid the small-pebble complex by feeling a sense of participation in a process he fully understands. Each worker is encouraged to find improvements for production technology—possible new instruments (like a recent electric screwdriver with a unique counterweight attached), methods of saving time, and avoiding common errors. Rapport is maintained not by ball teams but by workshops and discussions; down-to-earth plant newspapers are distributed once a month. There is perhaps even more communication today, between unit chiefs and assistant supervisors, then down to the line worker—conferences and subconferences that would drive American managers to hair-pulling but which build links and understanding at Sony. The honor system remains, still self-controlled by the employees, stronger today than ever before; motivations are still more voluntary, more spontaneous, less formalized, less ordered from the top than in the United States or in other Japanese firms. Some employees, on their own initiative, have made exquisite paper dolls and given them to the switchboard operators to brighten their working area. There is a big field day at most plants, perhaps a bazaar, festivals, an auction, basketball and volleyball teams—but the interest is generated by the employees; at Inazawa, an informal worker organization collects 200 yen a month in dues from each employee for these activities; the company does not subsidize these events.

It does sponsor, though, a creativity contest patterned closely on one first developed at Honda. Employees are encouraged to submit detailed plans and estimated costs for any scientific innovation with practical applications, not necessarily in the electronics field. The top twenty or thirty are singled out in a preliminary selection process, and up to $1,000 is provided for each to be made into a working model. Prominent entries in the first contest, judged by Morita, Ibuka, and several workers at Atsugi last autumn, included a "Gas-saving Meter" that tells a driver at what speed he is getting the best mileage from his gas; a sailboat that sails directly *against* the wind; a foot-propelled one-man helicopter (which barely got off the ground); a device for "Harnassing the Tides Coming into Tokyo Bay for Electric Power"; a "Super-expressive Projection System" for projecting images on train-tunnel walls; a curved

The new North Shore College in Atsugi.

temperature thermometer; and a free-form printed circuit board for use in nonflat items (this one has been adopted). The winners may only get a gold or silver egg (representing the embryo of an idea) but the program promises to become an invaluable morale-building concept.

Until recently, the need existed for a high school to which the junior-high graduates could go; now there are more high-school graduates, so in 1974, at a cost of about $7 million for the building and land, Sony founded the two-year North Shore College, with Dr. Michio Hatoyama, former director of the Sony Research Center, as its head. This is another pioneering experiment. As technology in the plants became more and more sophisticated, Ibuka and Morita realized that more and more "engineer-minded" technicians would be needed. Senior engineers come from Sony headquarters to teach in the accredited college, and various defective products are used for study along with advanced equipment. The girls study "Living Science" to prepare them "to think scientifically about the living arts." As part of the accreditation requirements, liberal arts and a foreign language are taught; Morita is especially interested in the language programs to promote his new internationalism, but so far the "engineer-minded" technicians are not.

I had expected the plants to be grim—either overcrowded or superstreamlined and out of a futuristic novel. They are neither. I found vast, strikingly bright and open facilities where, amid the noisy rattle, the rise and squeal of sound waves, snatches of music, the silent movement of conveyors like tiny ski lifts carrying the picture tubes, the spirit seemed exceptionally high, the care meticulous. Excellence remains a central requirement at all Sony plants. One prominent placard had this slogan in English: "Quality comes from a design and it must be built into products in the processes."

To my untrained eyes they seemed to be so building it in —with a vengeance. There were aging rooms where television sets were operated at 10 percent over voltage; some fifteen or sixteen inspection stations; a special quality inspection for the tubes that checked twenty-seven different characteristics in twenty seconds, and automatically recorded the results; a 10 percent random sample, where sets were subjected to especially severe temperature, humidity, and reliability tests—and some actually dismantled. Until the random sample is approved, no sets from a lot are shipped.

Some of these plants have come into being with startling speed; groundbreaking for the Ichinomiya plant took place on January 10, 1970, and by May 7 of that year, production had begun. While waiting for final government approval to build the Inazawa plant, not only were all plans and blueprints fully developed but earth-movers and tractors actually surrounded the property and, when authorization came on July 1, 1969, moved in within minutes; as soon as one section was completed and its roof in place, production equipment was assembled; in five months the plant was completed—and three days later the first tubes came off the line.

But while pressing to bring more than 100,000 tubes a month off the line, or managing 1,400 workers, or coordinating the production of a U-Matic that takes 5,000 parts and nearly 70 people to assemble, Sony has also kept a close eye to the people problems of modern industrialization. The textile in-

Left, Trinitron tubes on a conveyor belt at Osaki, 1969. *Above,* a Trinitron assembly line at Osaki, 1969.

Two Trinitron adjustment stations on the line at Osaki, 1969.

Packaging Trinitrons, Osaki, 1969.

dustries near Ichinomiya feared that Sony's new plant would pull away its workers—so Sony refused to interview textile workers. Many of the available workers were housewives, so the plant developed schedules that enabled the women to come in late (after they had seen their children off to school) and to leave early (in time to fix dinner); they were told, "You're housewives first; even stay out if necessary, but let us know in time so your colleagues won't be overburdened." (The plant has one of the lowest absentee rates in Japan.) Ichinomiya managers found that the area residents were by nature highly reticent, so they started discussion groups and invented a variety of "gaming problems" to draw the women out, so they could express their particular needs. One arresting practice at this plant is that every new employee (even the clerks and future managers) must spend a minimum of three months on the production line, with soldering iron and electric screwdriver, learning exactly what this plant does. Sumio Sano, a law school graduate who is now in charge of financial public relations for Sony Corporation in America (and helped Sony get its listings on the major stock exchanges), remembers spending several months on the assembly line in Osaki when he first joined the firm. This is fairly standard practice.

Though excellence in a product was the goal, management stressed that an individual alone could not make a product; if outstanding ability was rewarded too conspicuously, even at Sony, this became a detriment to general morale and destroyed the idea of the team. A slightly larger bonus might be given, or a symbolic prize or award, and such a worker might even be given a promotion to a position of more responsibility, but as many efforts are made *not* to single out the individual at this level.

Today, Ichinomiya, like a number of other Sony plants, operates autonomously as a wholly owned subsidiary. This makes it a separate profit center, of course, but it also enables local managers to make the day-to-day decisions only they could make; it gives the plants greater flexibility, allows them to function more as separate, decentralized units; and it avoids the time lost if decisions had to be made in Tokyo. Chiefly, though, this decentralization is an important step toward solving the problem of size: Sony will continue to grow but its autonomous units, supplying separate services, with different personnel and different local needs, will remain at manageable sizes.

There are various other kinds of flexibility built into the plants as well. A hundred-yard conveyor belt can be cut every ten yards and restructured rapidly to meet special order requirements; the number of lines used can be modified; and many workers know several processes and can be switched when so required—or to keep them interested. Though employees cannot be fired, when production needs change, total personnel can be adjusted by not hiring new workers and by allowing natural attrition to take its toll—or by shutting down lines and transferring workers to other jobs.

Today, Sony attempts to mediate deftly between the demands of *amae* and *jibun*. Lifetime employment remains an accepted fact, and Ibuka and Morita are aware that such security for the workers has its virtues: Japanese still feel a sense of responsibility for those below them and those below still expect certain perquisites from those above; and the security works both ways. This is likely to remain so for many years to come. But the executives and all the plant managers at Sony are especially committed to developing, along with teamwork and a sense of connection, independent thought and individual responsibility.

"The great question," says Kobayashi, leaning far back in his chair, closing his eyes tightly, puffing slowly on his pipe, "is how to keep communication among the cells, how to maintain all the links and let each employee know that he is *not* a small pebble. So many discontinuities are possible." Then, opening his eyes and leaning far toward me: "But that is the great problem for the world, too, isn't it? It is a great challenge —and experiment—and Sony remains a highly experimental company."

CHAPTER SIX

Managing Innovative Managers

*Sony is flexible in its operations as it is organized
by kinetic instead of potential energy.*

—AKIO MORITA

PETER DRUCKER, the renowned management expert, speaks
of Sony and a handful of other international firms as being
so innovative in their management policies that, rather than
having to motivate their employees, they are kept "too busy
finding the manpower and the money to run with the innovations their own organizations force on them."

Where does such rare spirit come from?

It begins at the top. It starts, at Sony, with Morita and
Ibuka—what they are, what they have done, and, I think, what
they say. Several executives spoke to me with affectionate
whimsy about the "analects of Morita and Ibuka." They are
the stuff that promotional brochures are made of: but they

represent a vision far deeper than slogans. The aphorisms that flit naturally through the many talks and articles by these two men are living concepts at Sony: They affect and invigorate the entire firm. Sometimes, in their Yankee-Oriental wisdom, these men sound like visionary capitalists who have closely studied the laconic maxims of Emerson and Confucius.

> **"Never follow others; blaze a trail and open up new areas where no one has ventured."**
>
> **"Sony leads, others follow."**
>
> **"We do what others don't."**
>
> **"Study yourself, think yourself, judge for yourself, and carry things out yourself."**
>
> **"There may be a limit to man's ability but there is no limit to his efforts."**
>
> **"Nothing is happier for a man than to do work that he enjoys."**
>
> **"It is your own task to wake up your sleeping talent."**
>
> **"Each person should be conscious that a man's worth lies in his ability."**
>
> **"Everyone has a desire to do some creative work. Presenting a theme for study, fostering interests, and encouraging true ability are jobs for the executive."**
>
> **"*A right man in the right place* is a slogan for yourselves, not for your boss. *You* should find the right place yourselves."**

Sen Nishiyama, an adviser for the American Embassy, was invited by Ibuka, who had known him since the war, to work for Sony.

"What kind of position is open?" Nishiyama asked.

Ibuka said: "I don't know, but we'll find something."

"That's a heck of a job to offer a guy!" said Nishiyama. But that, quite often, is exactly what Sony does: They hire a capable, perhaps promising person, then find the most challenging job for him to do. This was clearly the case with Suzuki, Unoki, Ohga, and many others I spoke with. As Sony expanded in the mid-1950s, it broke sharply with Japanese tradition by "raiding" and by running a series of half-page ads that insisted: "The seniority system and the stress on school background keeps young, able businessmen from demonstrating their abilities and aspirations. . . ."

In his book *Never Mind School Records* (a best seller that caused a furor when it was published in the mid-1960s), Morita says that even if a person has a degree in electrical engineering, once he is hired, management will rapidly try to discover what his real ability is; if he is especially skilled or suitable in other areas, he is so shifted. "The able person gets saddled with a tremendous amount of work," says Higuchi. "He is pushed hard. In that sense, we operate on a performance-and-ability center type of management that is quite different from that in other Japanese firms." Thus, the first seminal principle in Sony management is that able people are hired for what they are and will be, then goaded and pushed rather than contained. Hiring policies, whether for experienced or fledgling managers, focus on *expected* abilities. Then, after two years, the school records of all new employees are completely ignored: They are on their own.

Having hired a *person* (rather than filled a position), Sony often subjects them immediately to broad cross-training. Engineers and scientists must work in sales (some Ph.D.s have even worked behind a counter), salesmen and even law school graduates have worked on the production line in Sony factories. Some young managers are given scholarships for further study, perhaps at Columbia Graduate School, or sent abroad to learn internationalism in America, England, France, or Germany. If possible, the person is shifted every two or three years. Such rotation not only expands the breadth of a manager's knowledge, but also enables him (and top management) to discover the suitable job for a person and his most effective ability for the company. The result is well-placed managers who are not mere specialists but widely knowledgeable specialists.

Such training is expensive. An American company would want results more quickly, and an American employee would feel insecure if he did not produce some substantial results right away. But at Japanese firms in general, where employees are expected to remain with their company for a lifetime, such time and money is an investment. At Sony, it breeds both loyalty and the pride of achievement.

"Ultimately," says Morita, "the best way to train a person is to give him authority. Without authority and responsibility, it is difficult to make a man improve himself. We tell our young managers: 'Don't be afraid to make a mistake. But make sure you don't make the same mistake twice.'"

Morita gave Suzuki authority when he founded Sonam. He also gave Hajime Unoki exceptional authority when the man was quite young and inexperienced. Unoki had been with Sony only a month after he left a petroleum company, and was reading over mountains of letters received in the Europe and Africa section, when Morita called him late one evening. He had seen neither the president nor the general manager of his previous company in more than five years of employment, but though he was only in his late twenties, Morita had personally tried to persuade him to join Sony. "The very fact that top management could be so interested in a young kid was probably why I joined," Unoki told me. When Morita called that night, he told Unoki, "Our European salesman is sick. I need you to go to Africa."

Unoki protested: "I'm only a newcomer here. I don't even know what kinds of products we manufacture."

"That's all right," Morita quipped. "You can learn on the plane."

The trip, which took six months, led Unoki to South Africa, Nairobi, Ethiopia, East Africa, Sudan, Nigeria, Uganda, Dakar, and Mozambique. What he hadn't learned on the plane, he learned in dozens of African offices. He made market surveys to determine the best way to distribute in a given country and the proper companies to serve as distributors. He laid the groundwork for Sony's first major penetration into the difficult and underdeveloped African market. Eventually, he helped those countries that had insufficient money to buy complete units to develop facilities for their own production or assembly. "To get into some of the countries," he says, "we had to provide facilities or technology that would help them develop their own industrial power." As a result, Sony now has an excellent relationship with many of the developing countries. As the costs of labor and transportation swept higher, it became more and more prudent to move the factories to the marketplace than, as Unoki says, "to pay money to transport the air inside television cabinets." He sought and found distributors and agents who wanted the challenge of assembling and selling Sony's new and different products—and he began to spread Morita's concept of educating the market.

After Africa, Morita sent Unoki to the United States in 1963 for ten years. He was a door-to-door salesman on Long Island ("with very limited success"), then advertising manager of Sonam, working closely with Sony's ad agency on the micro-television ads. He served as branch manager first in Chicago, then in New York. Today, back in Tokyo, he is in charge of international marketing, and has the broad knowledge and experience to support this extremely crucial area of the Sony operation. More important, perhaps, is the fact that he had been led to assume and bear large responsibilities.

The business history of Norio Ohga is perhaps the most outstanding example of how Morita's ideas of creating innovative managers work.

When Ohga had first seen the tape recorder brought by Kurahashi to the Tokyo Academy of Arts, he realized its importance immediately. He was a sophomore then, just twenty years old, but he knew that this instrument could become as essential to vocalists and musicians as the mirror is to the dancer. Though he persuaded the president of the university to buy one of the units for 138,000 yen, he told Morita and Ibuka, in no uncertain terms, that their product did not produce sound of performance quality; the fact that he had no training in science did not prevent him from giving them *his* specifications for improvement, nor from sending them sketches for possible new designs.

In 1953, on the day he graduated, he went to Ibuka's office again and Ibuka said: "I know you will be pursuing music and studying further but we would like you to become a part-time contract adviser."

Ohga was so astounded by the offer that he left his diploma by mistake in Ibuka's office. But he accepted. He did not think the little work he would do for them would interrupt his musical career. He had many concerts that year, became a vocalist for the NHK Symphony Orchestra, sang in *Don Giovanni* and *Tannhäuser,* then spent three years studying in Germany. "In my wildest dreams," he told me, "I never thought I would work for the company full time."

Morita wrote him regularly when he was in Europe, and Ohga, in return, sent on his own ideas and interesting articles he had clipped from German radio magazines. Once Ibuka went to Europe for a conference with Telefunken, and had to burst out laughing when the outspoken Ohga—serving as interpreter, guide, and driver—vigorously entered the high-level discussion himself.

When Ohga returned to Japan in 1957 he began a series of recitals and opera appearances whose fine reception assured him that he could pursue a highly successful career in music. He had married a fine concert pianist, and neither of them seriously considered that Ohga would ever leave music.

But Morita kept after him.

When Sony decided to expand its European sales in 1958, Morita persuaded Ohga, then twenty-eight, to survey the market for him. Morita arrived a month later and soon afterward the two men left Southampton together on the S.S. *United States,* bound for New York. It was a fateful trip. Sharing a small cabin together for four days, with little else to do, they talked and argued ten or twelve hours a day about electronics. Finally Morita burst out with it. "Look," he said, "I realize you are an excellent artist but you could be an extraordinary business-man. And this is what you ought to be."

Ohga wasn't to be convinced.

His wife opposed the idea constantly.

Then, some weeks later, Morita and his wife invited the Ohgas to dinner. The entire evening, at one of the best restau-rants in Tokyo, was an unabashed act of persuasion, topped off by Morita's assertion (which proved untenable) that Ohga could come aboard full time and still sing.

On October 1, 1959, Ohga joined Sony full time and promptly became general manager of the production division, with special responsibility for broadcast tape recorders and other broadcast equipment.

"But you couldn't have had any experience in *produc-tion*," I protested.

He shook his head.

"None?" I asked.

"None." His pudgy hands went out at his sides; a broad grin filled his dark-complexioned face. "This is Sony."

I asked Morita about the decision, and was told: "He was very, very bright and I knew that he would be a brilliant businessman."

How did he know? Ohga had neither science nor business training; he knew nothing about production.

"If you're bright in one way, it can usually be used in other ways."

Ohga proved himself a highly aggressive and capable manager. The way Sony could overtake one of its chief com-petitors, he reasoned, was to win away their sales manager; he did so and the next year the market share was reversed, in Sony's favor. He says: "I spent a lot of my time after that raid-ing other companies. This was essential for Sony at that time— and many of the men I hired are now the top managers." When he showed special interest in tape recorders, Ibuka put him in charge of the entire tape recorder division—in which Sony still maintains the largest market share in Japan. When he insisted upon developing automatic level adjusters in the early 1960s, even Ibuka objected at first—but Ohga persisted and soon Sony came out with such a device, which quickly helped the wide popularization of tape recorders.

Ohga also proved himself a shrewd negotiator. When he realized the advantages of the new cassettes over the reel-to-reel tapes, he knew that cassettes should be standard throughout the world. Philips already had a cassette, and Telefunken, Gründig, and Sony began to discuss the possibility of working out a new standardization together. Then a Philips representative came to Tokyo and suggested the advantages of using the Philips standard—at a royalty of 25 yen, about 7 cents, per cassette. Other companies were interested too, now, and scores of hard bargaining sessions finally brought Philips down to two cents a cassette. Matsushita signed at that rate but Morita said: "We must not have to pay that royalty."

Ohga agreed.

He went back to Philips and told them about his talks with Telefunken and Gründig. If they decided on a different standard, with the substantial world-market share they commanded, they could destroy Philips's hopes for standardization of their cassette. "We will not agree to a payment of two cents," Ohga said. "But if you allow us to do this free, we will go along with your cassette, which will then definitely become the standard."

A year later, Sony and Philips signed a royalty-free cross-licensing agreement that included Sony's all-automatic level-control recording device and the Philips cassette. The cassette and the level-control device are what finally assured the widespread boom in tape recorders in the 1960s.

After only five years, at the age of thirty-four, Ohga was made a board member. By this time he had assumed exceptionally wide-ranging responsibilities. At his insistence, Sony had incorporated the microphone into the body of the tape recorder—another first; he had been in charge of radio and television planning, then was put in charge of *all* product planning. When he argued that no matter how well a product was planned, unless the outward appearance was exceptional, it would not sell, top management put him in charge of industrial design. When he began to advise them, gratuitously, that no matter how good a product was, or how well it was designed, it would not sell unless properly merchandised and advertised, they said: "All right, you are in charge of those, too."

Because of his success in the Philips negotiations, Morita chose Ohga to be the chief negotiator, with Rosiny, in the talks with Harvey Schein, Goddard Leiberson, and Walter Yetnikoff about the formation of CBS-Sony in 1967. Each company put up $1 million in capital to begin the venture for distributing recordings in Japan, and agreed to take 1 percent of the gross off the top each year. Ohga has been president of this joint venture since its inception. It is so successful today that not only has the company no outstanding debt—unheard of in Japan—but is able to borrow at minimal rates because of its strong position and then loan money out at a higher rate.

Ohga remains the prime example of just how much work Sony will feed its ablest managers. Along with his recent appointment to the post of deputy president, he has assumed so many other responsibilities at Sony that he can now spend only half a day, Thursday morning, as president-in-residence of CBS-Sony, perhaps his most abiding love.

Despite such radical encouragement of individuality, Sony shares some of the traditional features of Japanese management. Lifetime employment is a fixture, the pay scale is at least partially determined by seniority (many able young men are indeed "saddled with a tremendous amount of work" but are neither given a higher title nor more pay), even top executives wear the navy-blue company jacket (with Sony embroidered over a top pocket) and an identification card, in the offices there is considerable bowing and green tea, and a "godfather system" is generally employed.

The latter—by which a superior is expected to concern himself with the needs, expectations, and training of a young manager—produces interesting results. Mike Morimoto, an exceptionally able manager at Sony's San Diego plant, would meet every morning from 8:00 to 8:30, for about seven years, with Higuchi. He developed "total respect" for the man, and was so well trained not only in the specific work he was doing but in many general managerial duties that when a problem comes up today, he often asks himself: "If Mr. Higuchi were in my position, what would he do?" Sumio Sano worked closely with Yoshii for many years in establishing the listings for Sony stock on exchanges throughout the world; he is now a highly skillful link to the New York stock analysts, and is so well trusted by top management that he can get *any* information about the company he wants. This apprentice system encourages constant communication between all levels of management, which is a special emblem of the Sony system—but chiefly it enables younger men, who eventually may assume high authority, to watch top management in action from close range. I wish there were more of this in America.

"When our company name was Tokyo Tele*communications*," says Morita with a smile, "I realized that we ought to start communicating *inside* the firm first." This was not easy. The Japanese are, by nature, quite formal, conforming, hesitant to express themselves; they worry constantly about saving face. But "the will to work depends very much on the feeling of personal participation," says Morita. "Even if it takes some time, an employee who acquires a feeling of personal participation in a decision performs much more effectively than one who merely is given a one-way order." With individual responsibility not too carefully defined, and the organizational chart down played, managers learn to help out where their talents are required. The *nature* of a mistake is determined but rarely is the culprit formally named, which would embarrass him, cause him to lose face and motivation. The Japanese concept of *nemawashi* (cultivating the ground for the roots to develop) encourages younger managers to become involved with the basic elements in any decision; ideas come from below and laterally, and the famous *ringi*, or consensus, system enables everyone to contribute. "Very often," says Morita, "Japanese leaders who express themselves only very vaguely are actually those who have superior talent in bringing everyone into the discussion and drawing out from groups in lower levels the consensus the leader already has in mind."

But isn't automatic tenure a serious impediment? What happens when a person is *not* Norio Ohga?

Morita says that this is not the man's fault but management's for wrongly hiring him. "We feel responsibility to carry such people for life," he says. "It is most important to keep our capable people and not too expensive to carry those who are less so." Also, there is built-in flexibility. Such people can be shifted to positions of less authority; at age forty-five a decision is usually made whether or not a person is top-management material; if not, he will be retired at the official retirement age of fifty-five.

When he first started doing business in the United States, Morita thought it a fine thing that incompetent employees could be fired. Then he got a shock. He had instructed a Sonam sales manager thoroughly in his basic concepts of marketing, sent him to Japan for further (and expensive) study and training, and then, when the man had become "top notch," he quit and went to work for one of Sony's chief competitors.

"Then," said Morita, "I realized the American system might not be so good."

"Japanese companies," he says, "have been trying to promote loyalty and the my-company concept by supplying employees with fringe benefits—company houses, dormitories, hospitals, summer houses, recreation facilities, and so forth. Although such fringe benefits have contributed to a uniquely

Japanese familylike feeling among employees, they tend to make employees forget the true purpose of business."

Even at the higher levels, Morita does not choose to "buy" his managers with such sweets. He insists on motivating them by giving them joy in their sense of achievement; maximum challenge, pride in what they do; recognition of their efforts; and a sense of mission. Teamwork and cooperation are essential—"like in an ancient castle, all the odd-shaped rocks must fit"—but individual talent is widely encouraged. The firm and its managers must be capable of "rapid change and reorganization" but there must be a constant two-way sense of loyalty.

Loyalty.

Perhaps that is the rarest trait of all. One knowledgeable and tough-minded American manager, who had come to Sonam after ten years in another company, put it this way. "At meetings, no one comes in with a muffler. We argue and debate as strongly and as loudly as we can; but when we come out, we all sing off the same song sheet." Then, pointing to his heart and head: "So much of what Sony means to us is here and here. It's difficult to describe. We all *feel* different and we know we are treated differently; we do business differently. We are given responsibility and encouragement. Our opinions count. It is a feeling you get about this company. Sometimes you are afraid to say it: It sounds like it's dipped in honey. But it's here. In my wildest flights of fancy, I don't think of leaving Sony."

I haven't heard that song sung in America too often lately.

CHAPTER SEVEN

The Tummy Television and Other Bold Anachronisms in America

In the United States . . . market research is conducted only to provide the man in charge with a rationale when a product flops, or when it succeeds.

—AKIO MORITA

MORITA FREQUENTLY tells a story about two shoe salesmen who, in their travels, find themselves in a rustic, backward section of Africa. The first salesman wires back to his head office: "THERE IS NO PROSPECT OF SALES SINCE ALL THE NATIVES ARE BAREFOOT." The other, reflecting Morita's concept of marketing, reports: "NO ONE WEARS SHOES HERE. WE CAN DOMINATE THE MARKET. SEND ALL POSSIBLE STOCK."

"We don't believe in market research for a new product unknown to the public," says Morita. "So we never do any. We are the experts."

Bold words.

The world's first all-transistor television, TV-8-301, marketed in Japan in May 1960 and in America in June 1961.

Nowhere in the history of Sony, and rarely in other industries, has there been such a classic example of this as the marketing of the transistorized television Sony developed in 1959 and marketed in America in the early 1960s.

After Sony perfected the transistor radio, it immediately turned its attention to the development of transistorized television. No one in the world had yet been able to do this. In America silicon transistors were produced for various industrial and military uses, but these cost up to $50 each—and few people conceived that they could be made for commercial use. Slowly, Ibuka and his semiconductor experts improved the transistor to handle the one to two hundred megacycles required for television frequencies, to provide the required deflection power to sweep the electron beam over an adequate angle and distance. By 1959 they had done this—a world's first —and along with the high-powered silicon transistors they also devised new components. (Those in existing television sets were made to fit with vacuum tubes.) While working on this project, though, they discovered that they could not yet get enough power to drive the large picture tubes: What they had produced was applicable only to very small tubes.

Would small, portable television sets—like pocketable radios—sell?

Most marketing experts in the United States thought not. RCA had tried to sell a set with a 7-inch screen, using vacuum tubes, but they had found it virtually unmarketable. People wanted larger and larger sets, everyone thought. Earl "Mad Man" Muntz was pushing a mammoth 27-inch set; some manufacturers were putting a magnifying glass over the screen to make the image larger. Sony decided to make an 8- and also a 5-inch set, for which they had to produce their own new cathode-ray tube. This represented another major risk.

The market experts said: "Absolutely not. There is no way it will sell. It is financial suicide. Everyone wants elaborate consoles with *huge* screens."

In the early 1960s, after they had announced the micro-television and established Sony of America, the company struggled to meet its quotas and to expand into the American market. Sonam headquarters at 514 Broadway, that long narrow office in the back of the building, were so shabby that Ira Morais, a novice public relations man, was at first disinclined to take them on as clients (though he did). It is reported that the warehouse superintendent had to come into the seedy building early every morning with a .22 rifle to shoot the rats, and that Morita—when he was in the city—frequently swept out the offices himself. One American employee recalls: "In the summer the air conditioner never worked, in winter the heater started on Wednesday."

But they scarcely noticed.

Suzuki says of those first seven months: "We had never distributed before in our lives. We didn't even know how to price our products. I had been in the Japanese army and knew what it meant to go all out, even to risk your life; but I worked harder in New York and I can remember no experience so impressive." Hiroshi Okochi, a Sony salesman en route to Japan from Europe, was snatched up and put to work establishing a sales network. Later, Yoshitami ("Tom") Arai, an interpreter guide with the U.S. State Department, was enlisted; Kazuya Miyatake, the graduate student at Columbia who helped move all those radios, was yanked out of school permanently and made warehouse manager. Morita stayed for one week in February, then flew back to Tokyo, then returned in early March.

Sagor says: "However busy he was in those days, Morita could tell you at a moment's notice the precise shipping schedules around the world." He was still such a flurry of activity, racing up and back the long row of desks after Sonam took over the Agrod offices, that the American and Japanese employees bought him a fireman's hat for his birthday.

Every night Morita phoned Tokyo; one call brought three service engineers; others followed soon, for both Morita and Ibuka strongly believed in establishing proper servicing *before* a sales network.

Saturday was a regular workday for the Japanese in Sonam. Many worked daily until late at night. "Twelve midnight was par," says Suzuki, "but often we worked until one or two." Suzuki and Morita would finish a long day's work, often having missed dinner, and then usually eat in a little delicatessen across the street. "I became very familiar then," Morita told me with a smile, "with matzoh ball soup." And much later, "when those bread ads began to appear in subways," he remembered those meals and told himself: "You don't have to be Jewish to love corned beef sandwiches and matzoh ball soup."

"We are selling diamonds," Morita told his staff. "Real diamonds. We are not selling cheap paste that you can buy in the five-and-ten-cent stores. We must pick the right kind of stores for our products." Some of the selecting was done for them. They had to raise their prices above those Delmonico had charged, and they decided to standardize the prices at which their products would be sold to dealers. Some of the dealers were surprised; they had assumed that now that the manufacturer was distributing, the price would come down.

Okochi, working with Milton Thalberg from the Agrod organization, began by developing sales networks centered in a few large cities first—New York, then Los Angeles, then San Francisco, Chicago, and Dallas. In three months, with still only a skeleton staff, they had a sales network large enough to cover half the buying potential in the United States; their headquarters staff that June was only nine employees. But they had established and maintained their target of 6,000 radios sold a month —and were ready to increase their number of employees sharply.

Before Suzuki returned to Tokyo that first August, Morita handpicked Shigeru Inagaki as the man who would pilot and expand Sonam for years to come. Morita trusted Inagaki, who had lived in America for some years and had been his classmate; he gave him basic concepts and allowed him to work out the details.

By 1962, when Sonam was able to move its offices to 580 Fifth Avenue, Morita got the idea that he must live in America for an extended period of time. He knew now that America would be an extremely important market for Sony, and that top management should *know* this market, not merely through statistics but "by feeling." Ibuka and Iwama were shocked when he announced his decision. Morita was then executive vice-president of Sony; no Japanese company had ever sent such a high-ranking official into residence in America. Also, living in New York would represent a tremendous expense.

Was it worth it?

Morita told Ibuka: "This will be an important investment for the future. I *must* learn how Americans think and feel, and why they buy. We must go through this stage, to learn which products they will buy with which designs." (He had already departed yet again from tradition by beginning to design products specifically for the country to which they would be exported rather than marketing the exact model sold in Japan; this concept would become even more defined in coming years.)

Morita's wife, Yoshiko, was equally surprised; their three

children were disconsolate—until Morita promised them a trip to Disneyland.

Morita, deciding that his address would be important, rented a twelve-room apartment at 1010 Fifth Avenue, opposite the Metropolitan Museum of Art. Richard Halloran, commenting on the widespread insularity of Japanese, says: "They usually absorb little of the real life of the nations they visit." Morita told his wife: "We are not to limit our friends to Japanese. I want to meet as many Americans as possible. I want to know them, so I won't be a stranger here."

A week after the family arrived in June 1963, the Moritas sent their two older sons, eight and ten, neither of whom spoke a word of English, to a summer camp in Maine. (The younger boy, unable to make his needs known, and shy, went without sneakers for two weeks.) For those first few weeks, when guests were not permitted to visit or call, the boys toughed it out, but by the time the Moritas arrived for their first visit, the boys didn't want to leave. When they returned to New York City, managing English much better already, they were sent to Saint Bernard's; their younger sister went to Nightingale Bamford.

The Moritas joined Edward Rosiny's country club in New City—like scores of other Japanese executives, Morita is passionate about golf—and began to attend a flood of operas and concerts in the newly opened Lincoln Center, and musicals. At first, Mrs. Morita could say only "hello" in English and then, perplexed, listen while the other person talked away in a language she could not understand. She got a driver's license and carefully mapped out destinations—to the country club, to Rosiny's home in Monsey, to Irving Sagor's home in Larchmont, to Dr. Esaki's home in Chappaqua (he had taken a job with IBM, to further his interest in computer technology), to Williamsburg, to a ski resort in Vermont; then she would put the children in the back of the car and head off. One wrong turn and she was fearfully lost.

But before long, the children had settled comfortably into American life and she too began to feel more at home, which is not surprising: Mrs. Morita is an attractive, animated, highly verbal woman.

In Japan it is customary to entertain outside one's home, on the notoriously lavish corporate charge accounts; but in America, with no cook and only one Japanese girl to help her, Mrs. Morita began a tradition she would eventually bring back to Japan, and even write a book about: home entertaining. She is an exceptional hostess—natural, warm, with an infectious little laugh and a rare capacity to make even very shy people feel very much at home—or at least became one in America. She estimates that during the eighteen months she lived on Fifth Avenue, doing all the cooking and most of the serving herself, she entertained at least 600 guests, most of them Americans.

This was an important year for Morita. He makes friends with exceptional ease, and genuinely likes them; and he made many important contacts. At Sonam, he loved to bring everyone together, Japanese and Americans, and talk with them about the company—its history and its hopes. Ken Nees, a young man who entered Sonam directly after college in 1962 and has since become both secretary and an assistant vice-president of Sonam, remembers how Morita stressed, even then, that Sonam was an *American* company and that he wanted to replace as many of the Japanese managers as he could as soon as possible, using Americans and American management techniques. Nees also speaks with great warmth about the enthusiasm Morita generated, his openness and genuine concern for all members of the firm. "He has an uncanny ability to know what everyone wants to know," says Nees. "He is always gracious. I have never seen him upset. I never saw him embarrass anyone. He wanted to know everyone in the firm and to create real two-way communication. I'll bet that today he would even know the warehouse manager at Moonachie, New Jersey, and ask him all about his family." (I could not resist asking Morita this, in Tokyo, and he said immediately, his face brightening, "Sure. Charlie Farr. We worked together at 514 Broadway.") Nees says: "He created an office where there is minimum politics and none of the guerrilla fighting common in American firms." Morita also encouraged a "matrix type of organization," similar to that in Japan, where everyone felt a part of the whole operation. "That structure creates loyalty," says Nees, "and a broad sense of responsibility. Technically, I am manager of administration, but it only begins there."

Morita's primary reason for coming to America was, of course, to sell Sony products. The headquarters staff moved to Fifth Avenue in 1962; that same year Morita had also decided that they should have a showroom to display Sony products. He and Kurahashi had developed the showroom concept in Tokyo, several years earlier. For customers to understand new products, they had to see them function. Morita commissioned the architect Yoshinobu Ashihara (who built the Komazawa Olympic Park in Tokyo and the Japanese Pavilion at Expo '67 in Montreal) to build the seven-story Sony building on a prominent corner in the Ginza. The building and land cost 3.2 billion yen (about $8.8 million). With its unique interior—continuous step-grade sections, like petals, with such renters as Fuji Film and Toyota—the conspicuous neon marquee at the top (which appears in so many photographs of Tokyo), the ground-floor display area for Sony products, and Maxim's de Paris of Tokyo (which Sony owns) in the basement, the building has proved a huge success. The New York showroom, which Morita personally designed, immediately attracted attention. He was still educating his customers; they could not buy what they did not understand, and a showroom created a perfect demonstration facility. Only in 1976—for economy and because adequate demonstrations were now possible in retail stores—was the New York showroom discontinued.

The showroom did much to generate interest in the 5-inch microtelevision that Sony brought to America in 1962. But the showroom was local.

Morita wanted a national campaign, one that would promote his products in all the major sales areas and establish the

The Sony building on the Ginza, Tokyo.

The Sony sign on Broadway. *Photo by A. A. Reiss*

Above, crowds in front of the Sony showroom, Paris. *Below,* the Sony show-room, London.

Sony name permanently in the minds of American consumers. He was ready, against all the market predictions, to back his new product fully. With more and more programs on the air, an increasing number of new channels, he reasoned that each person could now have his personal set. The microtelevision would *personalize* televiewing. He instructed his sales manager and his salesmen in the approach he wanted them to take; he began to find new uses for a portable television set. The RCA executives and "Mad Man" Muntz thought otherwise, but as always Morita was supremely confident.

The 5-inch Micro-TV, TV-5-303, first marketed in America in October 1962.

A later, smaller, and more sophisticated microtelevision.

He began to pay a great deal of attention to advertisements, and noticed that the Volkswagen ads were invariably interesting, amusing, strong; they had done a remarkable job of establishing the German-made car in America. He also marked other ads that struck him as similarly effective.

Who were the advertising agents for these campaigns?

At a PTA meeting at St. Bernard's, Morita met a man named Arthur Stanton, who knew Sony and proved to be the first American agent for Volkswagen in the United States. Morita immediately asked him who handled the VW advertising, and learned that it was the same firm that had created most of the other ads he had marked—Doyle Dane Bernbach.

Stanton set up a lunch between Morita and William Bernbach, and the two men at once got on well. Bernbach already knew Sony, which helped: He had walked past the Sony showroom many times (it happened to be near his office), and said he was impressed with the quality and uniqueness of the products displayed. He asked Morita for an estimate of their advertising budget; it would be only about $500,000 that year. Doyle Dane Bernbach rarely took on a new account with billing of less than $1 million—but because of his interest in Sony and his recent experience with Volkswagen, Bernbach would take them on. He *knew* the account would grow but chiefly he was interested in the nature of the products. Bernbach added: Not only would he handle Sony but he would assign his best people to the account, including the account executive who had worked on Volkswagen.

The ad read:

> **Tummy Television**   The 5 inch Sony, for waist sizes 38 to 46. . . . So that your wife can sleep, we also include a personal ear plug. The beauty of a TV set this small: when you've had a bellyful of television, you hide it under the pillow.

The picture showed a very content, quite plump, and bald gentleman tucked into his bed, an earplug tucked into his ear, a "tummy television" resting light as you please on his conspicuous tummy.

A top RCA official had insisted: We have spent millions on market research. *There is no market for such a small set.* Sony will bomb out.

He was wrong.

"Mad Man" Muntz's gigantic set with the 27-inch screen sold for under $150; this new little 5-inch set sold for $250. How could the Sony sell?

It did.

Tummy Television

The 5 inch Sony, for waist sizes 38 to 46. (For smaller tummies, buy the 4 inch set.) Our 32 non-heating, long-living transistors plus our telescopic antenna give you flicker-free reception—even if you jiggle when you laugh. The Sony works on AC wall plug or clip-on battery pack. So that your wife can sleep, we also include a personal ear plug. The beauty of a TV set this small: when you've had a bellyful of television, you hide it under the pillow.

Lightweight 5 inch SONY TV

Three of Doyle Dane Bernbach's finest.

Telefishin'

This might well be remembered as the first seaworthy television. It's the 9" Sony. (Not to be confused with sonar.) The Sony can't find fish, but the least we could do was include an earplug, so the noise won't scare them away. This Tackle-box-size TV operates on a rechargeable battery pack. And an AC wall plug for landlubbers. It has 29 little non-heating, long-living transistors. So you won't often be sending out "maydays" to the repairman. And even if the water gets a little wavy, the picture never does. Thanks to the 43" telescoping antenna. (To which you can also tie a white shirt. In the event you drift out too far.) And here's the best thing about it. When the fish aren't biting, you can always turn on the news. And catch Robert Trout. **The 9" Anyplace SONY TV**

The Walkie-Watchie

Son of Walkie-Talkie. But with pictures. (Unhappily, this new TV development is not a 2-way set like the Walkie-Talkie. But we *are* working on it.) It does *receive* brilliantly though. Thanks to its 32 little long-living, heat-free transistors and its flat-faced, non-distorting picture tube that doesn't show the scanning lines. For walking-watching it operates on a built-in battery pack and a built-in antenna right in the shoulder strap. (Some say the taller you are, the better the reception. But it's not so.) For sitting-watching, it has an AC plug that fits in your wall outlet and a directional telescopic master antenna. Turn on your Walkie-Watchie and *go*. You grown-up teenager you.

The 4 inch SONY television

Other ads followed:

Telefishin' This might well be remembered as the first seaworthy television. It's the 9″ Sony. (Not to be confused with sonar.) The Sony can't find fish, but the least we could do was include an earplug, so the noise won't scare them away.

Then some practical information, and the picture of barefoot man in sweatshirt, ball cap, and boat, the rod unattended, the Sony tuned in to a ball game. And a final pun in the legend: "When the fish aren't biting, you can always turn on the news. And catch Robert Trout."

There was even a 4-inch set, for the "Walkie-Watchie."

The ads did their work. With their droll wit, they caught attention at once; they were light—yet informative; they attracted the eye and held it. They didn't *really* ask you to put the set on your stomach and watch in bed, or on a boat, or walking, but they stimulated the reader to suggestions of his own. If not on a boat (where *no* self-respecting fisherman would take a television set), perhaps in . . .

Everyone else was simply saying "We're good. We have the best product. We have these ingenious features." Sony was taking that for granted: The humor drew you in, the differentness held your attention, you developed your own uses for the set, and you even found yourself asking for "a Sony"— not a television set. You never even knew Sony was a Japanese company. (So successful was this latter feature that *Fortune* reports *most* dealers said they never handled Japanese products —though a "majority sold Sony products.")

Ira Morais did his part, too, though at first he was up against severe obstacles. A national business magazine said of Morita: "He isn't big enough for us to send a man out to see him. Why don't you bring him over to our office to explain this new thing of his?" Morita willingly went, and the reporter got a prime dose of Morita's superb salesmanship. Not only

On June 8, 1973, Bob Yoder of the Amity Supply Company electronic store made a deposit at the First Federal Loan & Savings Association. In the window to be exact.

It was a 12"(diagonal) Sony Trinitron color TV.

On that date, the set was turned on. And it wasn't turned off until June 28, 1975, when it beat Sony's previous record.

It played continuously for 18,000 hours. Without repairs. Without adjustments.

The care that goes into the making of our sets, is why we're known for excellent perform-

ance. And this was one performance test an entire city got to watch and enjoy. Because rain or shine, that set stayed on.

And on the darkest, dreariest days of the year, the brightest spot in Pottstown was our picture (thanks to our one-gun, one lens Trinitron® system). Both color and picture were never less than perfect for each day of the 107 weeks it played.

At an average of five hours daily viewing time, the set would have run for almost ten years.

Let the bankers have their hours. Sony works overtime.

The longest running show in Pottstown, Pa.

OFFICE HOURS
MONDAY THRU THURSDAY
9:00 AM TO 5:00 PM
FRIDAY
9:00 AM TO 6:00 PM

ACTUAL CLOSED CIRCUIT PICTURE

"IT'S A SONY."

Ray Steiner once received a letter from a Pennsylvania bank president, informing him that a Sony TV had been in his bank's window, as the raffle prize for the local fire department, and that it remained on for an extraordinarily long time. Steiner, Dan Gallagher (the national advertising manager), and Doyle Dane Bernbach promptly devised and ran this ad.

did Morita understand this microtelevision perfectly but he had a dozen reasons why it would succeed; he was not a huckster but a man with total understanding of both his product and its market.

Morais was tenacious. During a Yankee World Series, he found a man waiting on line one morning for tickets, lent him a micro-TV, bought him breakfast, coached him about what to say, then called several television news reporters he knew. While he was waiting for them to arrive, he went back to the man and was assured: "I will remember. Sony. I will remember. Don't worry." But when the interviewers finally came and one asked, before the camera, "Where did you get the television set?" the man answered: "I don't know. Some guy came along here and left it." Morais threw up his hands, the interviewer smiled awkwardly—and said: "Well . . . it looks like a Sony."

Eventually, Morais's releases began to be picked up by many major newspapers and trade journals; articles on Sony began to appear in such magazines as *Reader's Digest, Business Week, Fortune, Time, The Lion;* he arranged countless interviews for Morita; and he even got Sony products onto the screen in such movies as *Errand Boy, Seconds, Cold Turkey,* and others. Sony was now the upstart, the newcomer; they always did things differently; they were glamorous—and promotable. Morais says: "The products made us look good."

The products were indeed becoming known—for their quality as well as their differentness. Someone at Mercedes-Benz said: "We like to be known as the Sony of the automobile industry."

Peter Drucker notes that if the *marketing* is successful, the selling is more than half done, the products presold. By 1969 Sony had sold its first million microtelevision sets in America.

When the "headhunter" who scouted out Ray Steiner for an open sales manager spot at Sonam told him, "I think I should tell you that I'm representing a Japanese company," Steiner wanted to say at once: "Sorry. I'm not interested."

Until the man said "Sony."

"Their reputation was already magnificent," he recalls, "but I didn't think they were yet a significant factor in the marketplace. I saw a real opportunity to contribute." It is obvious he did. He recognized at once the essential difference between Sony and other electronics manufacturers: "They see a market and come up with a product to fill it. Sony's philosophy is to develop a product when there is *no* market—and then create one." His contribution would be on the front line, where the actual sale is made—and for this he needed a first-rate sales force that could "educate as well as sell."

Steiner met and approved each new salesman, and personally went after and hired more than fifteen (none of whom has left to join another company). He sought "to get people who would be with Sony for the long pull, who would not take shortcuts or make a quick sale merely for the sake of a sale. We had high-priced Cadillac products, and couldn't afford to play a mere numbers game." Today there are over 250 Sony salesmen in America—fewer, Steiner says, than companies with comparable volume, but "well paid; they are not peddlers—they are highly professional."

He told his salesmen to seek dealers who would give Sony products a prominent display and be able to explain them well—and who would pay their bills—"quality merchants." He also realized that much of the electronics business was governed by "all sorts of wild deals." He wanted none of that. Sony products were especially high priced because of the large research and development costs and the added expense of severe quality control. "We have not bought anybody's business," Steiner insists. "We have one price sheet. We have one advertising deal. We have one program. We won't hassle. Dealers may not like our price sheet"—many, I learned, don't— "but we are committed to sell quality, not price."

Inagaki proved so conservative in his orders to Tokyo that there were always fewer sets available than Sonam could sell. From the time the first advertisements on the micro-TV broke in 1963, the company was back-ordered; they couldn't bring the sets in fast enough. Morita had created another market—and there was no immediate competition.

Japanese is so difficult a language that virtually none of the American executives could manage more than a few simple words. And beneath the surface of what seems a defined Westernization, says Halloran, "the essence of Japanese life flows from ideas, ethics, customs, and institutions that are anchored deep in Japanese culture and history."

I was particularly interested in how these two cultures worked together, what degree of understanding could be achieved; later, in San Diego, I looked at how Japanese management—or, rather, *Sony* management—worked in an American manufacturing plant.

"Relations with the Japanese take time," said one American executive. "They are very concerned in everything they do with being correct, not hurting someone's feelings." In the beginning some of the Americans would feel they had an understanding with Japanese co-workers; the Japanese would respond with a smile and say, "I see" or "Yes, yes," and then later the American would realize that no agreement had been reached. The Japanese had only thought, "I can embarrass this man by not understanding him, or by disagreeing with him." Some of the Americans found this and the Japanese penchant for discussion and consensus difficult to deal with.

Steiner told me he had been in the firm for six or eight months, being ultrapolite to an ultrapolite Japanese associate, before he said one day: "Goddamit, Heiro, we've got to have an understanding. When you come through that door, I don't have time to think that you are Japanese or American and I have got to treat you one way and the Americans another. I know we have different backgrounds, but get off the 'Mr. Steiner' stuff; from now on, you're Heiro and I'm Ray. If you're going to say something I disagree with, I'm going to say you're full of it. And if I say something you disagree with, you tell me the same thing."

Frankness.

That was the most difficult trait for the Japanese—who with their traditions of bowing, exchange of business cards, and subtle delineations of rank, sought to hide the self. The American often wears his self on his face; the Japanese contains, protects it.

Morita could be frank, and, increasingly, there were others. This too was pioneering—and Sony was no newcomer now to that trade.

The Americans and Japanese who worked in Sonam were becoming that bold anachronism—a truly international, unified team.

CHAPTER EIGHT

Not Merely Color But Better Color— The Trinitron

To move forward, a wheel must have torque, and it is intense and brutal competition that produces the necessary energy.

—MASARU IBUKA

AS EARLY as the mid-fifties in the United States and 1960 in Japan, color television sets began to appear on the consumer market. By 1964, they were already in widespread use—and it was readily apparent that the potential sales were immense; by the early 1970s more than 20 million sets would be sold in the United States alone.

Sony knew at once that it would have to venture into the lists. RCA had already developed its shadow-mask system and pioneered its use with great imagination: *All* color television manufacturers throughout the world, in fact, operate under their basic patent license. "I could see no fun in merely copying their excellent system," says Ibuka ingenuously, so

131

he decided to explore the possibility of an alternative, and perhaps better, system.

This decision too involved immense risk, or perhaps, as one American magazine suggested, "foolhardy courage."

This time Sony was years behind. It had recently concentrated its best energies on developing the transistorized microtelevision and as late as 1961 had no definite plans to enter the color market. But Ibuka knew they must try, and Morita already heard the grumblings of Sony dealers who realized they were missing an excellent opportunity.

At an Institute of Electrical and Electronics Engineers (IEEE) conference in New York in March 1961, Ibuka first saw a demonstration of the Chromatron tube invented in 1950 by Dr. Ernest O. Lawrence, the Nobel Prize-winning inventor of the cyclotron. Though the system, whose patent was owned by Paramount Pictures, was being used as a display screen for military purposes, to distinguish different obstacles, Ibuka was at once impressed. He was especially attracted by the picture brightness, reputedly three times brighter than that of the shadow mask.

Several months later he sent Susumu Yoshida to America to investigate the technological feasibility of the Chromatron. Yoshida had been recruited from an audio and radio company in 1953 by Norio Ohga, the young baritone who then served as a part-time consultant for Sony, and had worked in product development, on the transistorized television, and then the black-and-white television tube. Yoshida returned from America with an optimistic report and soon afterward Ibuka went back to America with Iwama for further study. The possibilities looked good: The picture was indeed bright and the product had not yet been adapted by anyone for consumer use. Ibuka had always valued such opportunities to find "unnoticed utility in others' inventions," then "seasoning them with original ideas" of his own to make new marketable products. The company still kept to its principle of "narrow but deep" specialization (rather than the diversification that, for

Ibuka, represented a form of defeatism); it could not afford to ignore the color market, which promised to become a central portion of its areas of specialty.

Sony secured a license under the Chromatron patent in 1962 and immediately launched an intensive program to develop its own tube.

For two years Sony engineers struggled with the concept. It proved extraordinarily difficult. Lawrence's basic system calls for one electron gun (rather than the three used for the shadow mask) with, as Ibuka says, "a beam to be controlled and focused on each color of the phosphor stripes after passing through a grid made of thin wires." The grille, at the face of the screen, requires an additional high voltage that will accelerate the beam after it is focused through the electron lens. Each metal line in the grid, representing one of the colors, is alternately switched on or off electrostatically. It is an extremely complex process, too complicated, they began to think, for mass production.

As they progressed, they decided to try three guns instead of Lawrence's one—one for each color; this did away with the sensitive and unreliable switching problem but retained the need for post-acceleration on the grid. There were other problems: The system was still too complex to produce easily—and extremely expensive. *If* the system worked properly, it produced an excellent color picture; but because of those delicate post-acceleration requirements, necessitating precise voltage on the grille, even a slight deviation produced color spills, color deviations.

By September 1964, they introduced the 17-inch Sony Chromatron color television, using vacuum tubes, and eventually sold 13,000 of them in Japan. But the more they made, the more defects they discovered. Servicing costs were tremendous, and many sets had to be replaced. "We kept spending more engineering effort and money," says Ibuka, "and the more sets we made, the more money we lost."

When Yoshida returned to America in 1966, the shadow

mask was firmly established; Sony was years behind its competitors and the market was being rapidly exploited. Key members of Sonam insisted that the firm *must* come out with a color television—and quick; and Yoshida was told by authorities in the field that though the sample Chromatron produced a good picture, Sony was too late with too little—and should switch immediately to the shadow mask. Yoshida, Ibuka, Iwama, and Morita considered the matter in depth. They had to admit the worst: The Chromatron was a disaster. It should not be marketed in America. They had sold only those 13,000 sets, and now it ought to be discontinued. The development work alone had cost about $700,000 a year. Technically and financially, it was not feasible.

They came to a hard decision: They would explore alternative systems for another year, and after that time, if they did not have a sure prospect for a good, reliable color system, they would disband the group of twenty top engineers who had been working in the color field and release them to the general staff for use on other projects.

There was no clear announcement that the Chromatron had been dropped but rather a vague period in which the engineers knew they had failed and that another system would have to be developed.

Sony had dropped other products abruptly and would do so again in the future. They were capable of investing millions of dollars in research and development, then—for technological or marketing reasons—dropping the product with remarkable speed. They made a wrist-watch radio (which one American called "a real turkey")—and dropped it. They developed a microtrain for electric toy-train enthusiasts, set up a special company to produce the item, and wrote it off. They developed a long-life mercury battery for radios, set up another new company, had an elaborate opening ceremony, then discontinued the product and sold the plant. They would be the first company in the world to produce an electronic desk calculator—and be out of that business before the plethora of pocket calculators flooded the market and initiated a price-cutting war. They would develop a Polaroid-type camera that recorded the subject's voice while he was being photographed, and then would find it unfeasible.

This was the risk of working on the outer edge. You could fail. Quite miserably.

Perhaps they should *not* enter the intensely competitive color television market after all.

Still, it was a major plum. There was no doubt by 1966 that the potential, if they found the right product, would beggar the imagination.

In the autumn of 1966, General Electric representatives approached Sony with a color system employing three electron guns *in line* (rather than in the delta configuration used with the shadow mask). Some staff members thought this might work, that the new concept might enable them to produce an innovation. They began to investigate the system thoroughly.

That year, research into an alternative method increased to a high pitch. Ibuka himself came to the laboratories every day, playing many roles, overseeing the work, making suggestions, participating in the actual experiments, always encouraging the men, giving them constant help and guidance. For the president of a firm with 8,000 employees to do this was unheard of.

He initiated a system whereby the engineers explored a large number of different alternatives, with the belief that they would select and ultimately develop the most successful. Then teams of engineers worked on these projects not in *series*—developing one stage, then going on to the next—but ran them *parallel,* selecting at each moment the road for each that seemed most promising and developing the ancillary technology to back each of these up. Ibuka switched the engineers from one project to another, working against time, juggling all the elements with deft speed.

Senri Miyaoka, a young man still in his twenties then, was working on one of the special teams under the general managership of Yoshida. "The fact that Ibuka, the very top man, was willing to be right there with us in the workshop," he recalls, "was a tremendous inspiration." Ibuka could, and did, talk man to man, as a fellow engineer; with Morita in charge of finance and marketing, Ibuka was free to talk technology, devote himself more and more to his deepest love—the development of new products. He had indefatigable strength and courage. They *would* find a way.

Miyaoka is an imaginative, witty, tenacious young man. His college professor had discouraged him from joining Sony, advising him to go to Matsushita instead; Sony had had its moment of glory with the transistor, the man said, but the day of the transistor was over. Miyaoka thought otherwise. He saw in Sony a chance to be innovative; he came in 1959 seeking a challenge. Now he had one—and it was nearly too much for him. Working with his team leader, Akio Ohkoshi, an intensely shy man who specialized in electrical circuitry, Miyaoka's spirit began to fade. All the engineers could see that the color television market was booming. The shadow mask system was highly successful, and they knew that with their technological skill and Sony's production capability, they could shift to that system at once; with the strength of the Sony name and its marketing network, they could have a comfortable share of the market within a year.

Instead, they were struggling with a system they could not master. The Chromatron had been a quagmire; Sony had lost a fortune on it—and the engineers felt personally responsible. Miyaoka remembers the sinking feeling he experienced with each paycheck or yearly bonus he received: He had no right to the money; his work was being paid for by the successes with tape recorders and radios.

By the autumn of 1966, when General Electric proposed the in-line guns, morale was at rock bottom. If this new system was adopted, some of the engineers felt that Sony would become nothing but a subcontractor for GE color picture tubes. This would be so alien to the Sony spirit, some thought, that they actually contemplated defecting to Toshiba, Hitachi, or Matsushita.

"No," insisted Ibuka. They would not use the General Electric system—though there was much they might learn from it; they would not use the shadow mask; they would not simply produce *any* color set because such a tempting market existed. Those alternatives would indeed be a betrayal. They *must* produce a new product, something of their own. "There is nothing more pitiable than a man who can't or doesn't dream," Ibuka has said. "Dreams give direction and purpose to life, without which life would be mere drudgery."

And it was chiefly this spirit, proceeding from one man, that galvanized the engineers to try yet again, to work harder and harder.

Morita, of course, was on the front line—and he faced a grave dilemma. He says he began to fear for the very financial stability of the company. All the dealers were now clamoring: "Where's your color television? Every other major electronics company has one. We're losing business every day—and we may never get it back. The market is becoming saturated."

Morita calmed them as best he could.

Every year, in January, Sony sponsors twelve regional gatherings throughout Japan of prominent Sony dealers. About three to four hundred dealers come to each, and Morita, always cognizant of the value of communication, speaks to each group for more than an hour. At such meetings during the color television crisis, Morita insisted that they were working on a new concept. "Business should be considered in ten-year cycles," he argued. "If we wait, and develop a unique product, we may start several years later but we can be stronger than all the other companies for the next ten years." In the long run they would make *more* money by waiting: Business should be determined by the "accumulation of profits" over such a ten-year period. It is like a marathon, he stressed: "Many start and many are ahead for the first few miles, but the man who keeps his own pace wins the race."

Had he not full confidence in Ibuka, he could not have made such statements. Every month more and more of the color television market was being sliced up. The strength of the company was being risked, but they all knew this was the only way they could go.

Toward the end of 1966, while running some experiments, Miyaoka made a mistake that produced some interesting results. Using the single gun, characteristic of the Chromatron, and three cathodes, he produced a blurred picture—but it was a picture, and by a new concept. He had time to run only a few experiments with the new arrangement and then, in his daily report to Yoshida, described his results. He was not at all sure of what he had made, and had little confidence that he could even produce an adequate picture let alone a technologically feasible unit.

Miyaoka, at twenty-nine, had one fixed commitment outside the company. Though he often worked late during the week, when the bell rang at four thirty on Saturday afternoons, he rushed off for community orchestra practice; he was an avid cellist. Somewhat after four on the Saturday of the week he had turned in his report on the one-gun three-cathode tube, he was urgently called to a special conference in Ibuka's office. Yoshida and Ohkoshi were there, too, and Miyaoka looked from one to the other, wondering vaguely why he was there and how long they would keep him.

"Now look," said Ibuka, holding Miyaoka's recent report. "What is your frank opinion about this new system? Do you think if we go with this, commit all our resources to it, it will really work? Will we get a better picture than the shadow mask?"

Miyaoka began to fidget.

He didn't really know. He had only run those few first experiments and they were inconclusive; he had only produced a blurred picture. He half smiled, half shrugged. He was in no position to give a flat answer.

Ibuka pressed him. "I'm not going to let you out of this room until you give me a 'Yes' or 'No' answer."

Miyaoka shrugged again, looked at his watch, and, in desperation, so they would let him go practice his cello, said "Yes."

Two days later, on Monday morning, Sony was committed to this new idea. When Ibuka first saw Miyaoka's report, he had analyzed it and told Yoshida immediately: "This is it. This is the system we ought to go with."

Yoshida had seen this in Ibuka before and was deeply impressed. "He has a genius," Yoshida says, "for being able to spot the right seed, for being able to see, almost instinctively, what will work and what probably won't. From the moment he saw that report, he targeted all our energies toward the development of that gun."

Miyaoka was terrified.

Had he led Sony into another Chromatron quagmire? He had no sure idea whether or not this new device could be made to work. But there was little time for worry.

Ibuka at once became the project team manager himself—and the development was accelerated further. All the other alternatives they had been working on were abandoned; all energies were focused on Miyaoka's chance discovery. The men worked with greater intensity now—and, under Ibuka's patient eye, with increasing confidence. Often they worked around the clock, taking several hours off in the dark early morning hours to rest on a sofa. Ibuka was always there—encouraging, steady, impassioned.

By February 1967 they had eliminated the blur and produced a decent picture with the new gun; many of the engineers thought it was already better than the shadow mask.

Now they had to decide whether to use the shadow mask screen, with its color dots, the Chromatron grid, or some new system.

After months of experiments on how to get the most accurate color reproduction on the screen, arguments, false trails, disappointments, in July they were on the verge, finally, of committing themselves to the single gun with three in-line cathodes that Miyaoka had initiated—and the old shadow mask screen. If the shadow mask was used with the new gun, the image looked very much like the regular shadow mask image— but with what seemed a definite improvement in quality; with the Chromatron grid, they got a better picture, but with many of the same problems of post-acceleration.

A week before the annual summer holiday, Ohkoshi proposed an entirely new concept: the aperture grille, made of vertical stripes by photoetching.

Ohkoshi's aperture grille was an attempt to combine the best features of the Chromatron grid with the unique features of the new gun. Its picture was markedly superior to anything any of them had seen, and it was easier to achieve. For the shadow mask, which has color dots, you must adjust both the convergence and the focusing of the direction of the electron beams to land on the dots in two dimensions, horizontally and vertically. The aperture grille had vertical color lines so you only had to adjust in one direction, horizontally.

But there were still serious problems.

"Though it was theoretically an excellent system," says Ibuka, "we saw at once that it would pose many technical production problems compared to the shadow mask."

When Ohkoshi first demonstrated it to Ibuka, he expressed grave concern that when the grille, stretched tight over a special heavy, firm frame, was heated, the picture would be distorted. Ohkoshi turned on a large incandescent lamp he had brought, and showed how the grille would sag when it got hot; when the heat was turned off, the grille would stretch again. Clearly, the metal strips would vibrate—expanding and contracting—as the electron beams hit them. There was also a distracting humming sound. None of the engineers had been able to solve the problem. On the Chromatron grid, the wires

The first Trinitron.

A diagram of the Trinitron gun—and its competitors.

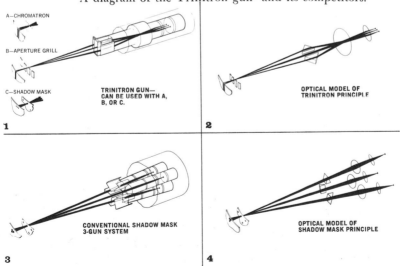

A—CHROMATRON

B—APERTURE GRILL

C—SHADOW MASK

TRINITRON GUN— CAN BE USED WITH A, B, OR C.

1

OPTICAL MODEL OF TRINITRON PRINCIPLE

2

CONVENTIONAL SHADOW MASK 3-GUN SYSTEM

3

OPTICAL MODEL OF SHADOW MASK PRINCIPLE

4

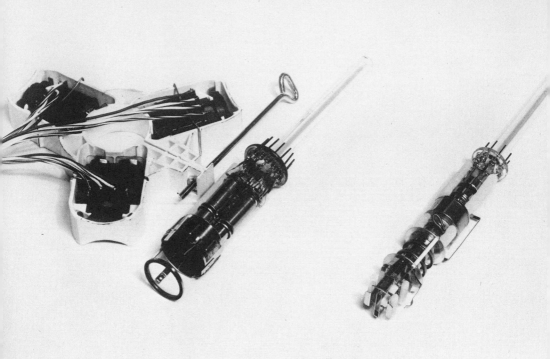

A conventional delta three-gun and its convergence yoke assembly *(left)*, and the Trinitron gun.

A conventional three-gun color tube and the Trinitron color tube.

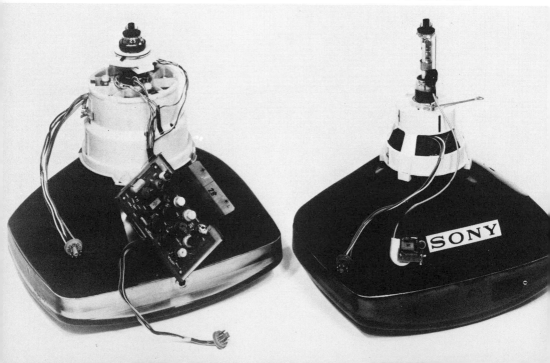

were interleaved with glass rods to prevent this shifting—but this would not work for Ohkoshi's grille.

Ibuka watched the demonstration carefully. He knew that the heavy frame would require special technology, and that the accurate etching of the colored lines on the glass picture screen would cause problems. Without changing his expression, he watched Ohkoshi's grille contract when the lamp went off and promptly said: "Oh, don't worry about that. We can solve that easily." Within a short time he himself devised two simple tungsten wires that, when stretched across the grille, held it firmly in place and prevented the sag and stretch; he also developed the final etching process.

One last problem remained. All television sets used a standard size glass envelope. Sony again had to persuade a component manufacturer to produce one of a unique size and shape for their new product. When they finally secured a manufacturer's cooperation, Yoshida took the super express down the coast to Shizoka Prefecture to pick up the first sample; he returned that evening. The engineers worked all through the night, and on the next day, October 16, Sony demonstrated its new color television—the Trinitron.

"The Trinitron," says Miyaoka, "was born as a direct result of those intensely trying times."

In April 1968, Ibuka officially announced the new color television system and, in a press release, without consulting the engineers, said it would be on the market within six months. Morita similarly announced the set in New York a month later.

Yoshida, who had previously worked only in the development division, was chosen to be in charge of production. He did not think it was possible. They needed more time. There was too much work still to be done.

But Ibuka brought the chief engineers together and told them to study the Manhattan Project—it would be a useful reference!

Yoshida established two teams, working parallel—one to develop the Trinitron into a commercial design, the other to establish the new production machinery and processes, with adequate quality control. Though the dealers had requested a 17-inch screen, Yoshida pleaded that they should make one first that was only 12 inches. In this they could have full confidence; they might have high-voltage problems with their transistor (the sets would all be solid state) and he feared there might be mechanical problems with the strength of the new glass envelope in the larger sizes. Though many American observers claimed that, since color images lose clarity and definition as they grow larger, this set was only brighter because it was smaller—and thus merely a brilliant marketing ploy—this factor had not influenced the decision to make a 12-inch set first.

Yoshida's biggest problem, he recalls, was convincing the production staff that the Trinitron would actually work. They had lived for more than five years with the unsuccessful Chromatron and there still lingered that sense of demoralization, the nagging feeling that, even after they had come so far, this system too would fail. Yoshida insisted this would not happen. Supported by Ibuka, who was there daily—arguing, watching, discussing progress and problems with even the youngest engineers—the Sony Manhattan Project began to gain momentum.

Sony bought what is now their Osaki plant, which had been a large machine plant, and began to punch holes in the floors to fit in the conveyor systems, move walls, design a production line. Engineers would be working at a desk for several weeks, find themselves displaced as new equipment was brought in or a hole punched in the ceiling above them, and scurry for a quieter corner; some remember moving eight or ten times. Stations were established for making the aperture grille, photoetching, preparing the glass envelope, inspecting and preparing the gun parts, inserting and sealing the gun, print-sealing around the edge of the envelope.

Receiving awards is a habit for Ibuka, who here accepts the 1972–1973 Emmy for "Outstanding Achievements in Engineering Developments" for the development of the Trinitron. Among other major honors he has received are: Director-General's Honor Award from the Japanese Science and Technology Agency (1959); the Medal of Honor with Blue Ribbon from the Emperor of Japan (1960)—which Morita was also awarded in 1976; the coveted Founders Award of the Institute of Electrical and Electronics Engineers. He was made a foreign member of the Royal Swedish Academy of Engineering Science in 1971 and in April 1976 was elected foreign associate of the National Academy of Engineering in the United States, the first time a foreign member has been admitted. In May 1976 Sony received a second Emmy, for the U-Matic VTR.

The staff would expand to as many as a hundred scientists and engineers at times, depending upon what work was needed —and the project had top priority—and then contract, with employees shifted to other assignments. Designing had to be completed. Equipment had to be ordered. New personnel had to be interviewed and hired. Assignments had to be made. Yoshitoshi Araki, an extremely thoughtful man who now serves as plant manager at Inazawa, remembers working *140* hours one week. His section of the Osaki plant had no windows and he rarely knew whether it was night or day; several times his new wife called him at 2:00 A.M., frightened, wondering why she hadn't heard from him.

And then, miraculously, the six months were up and Yoshida had actually produced the first sets for the market. It had cost Sony an estimated $12 million to develop the Trinitron.

Ten thousand sets were brought off the lines at Osaki by Christmas Eve, when Ibuka met privately with Yoshida, Shiro Yamada (who now runs the San Diego plant), and Araki. He looked at each of them for several long moments in silence. Then he said simply, "Thank you."

There were tears in his eyes.

The Trinitron was immediately successful. By March 1969, Sony plants were producing 10,000 sets a month; by autumn the number had jumped to 20,000. Within two years the Trinitron commanded the biggest market share in the small-screen color television market in Japan.

Ibuka saw that Miyaoka, Ohkoshi, and Yoshida shared in the many awards the Trinitron earned. He himself went to California to accept an Emmy for the innovation—the first time such an honor was bestowed on a product.

By 1976, ten years after Morita had spoken of his ten-year concept, Sony had sold 10 million sets—and expected to produce 1.8 million that year. They have still not been able to catch up with the world demand for the Trinitron.

CHAPTER NINE

Seeds and Fruit

We shall create our own unique products . . .
with a determination that other companies cannot
overtake.

—MASARU IBUKA, 1946

If research bear a true fruit, the research must start
from needs.

—MASARU IBUKA

S O-ICHI OHYA, the late Japanese essayist, once called Sony a
"guinea pig industry" because it was always experimenting with nontraditional methods of management, personnel
relations, and marketing, as well as new product development.
A lot of employees reacted sharply to this at first, taking it to
be one of the acid insults for which Ohya was so famous. But
Ibuka said: "That's perfect. We *are* what he says. That's exactly what we are doing." In 1960, when Ibuka was awarded

147

the Medal of Honor with the Blue Ribbon by the Japanese government for his contributions to Japanese industry, Sony employees gave him a metal guinea pig mounted on a wooden base. It was sculpted by Anso Mitsui, a professor at the Tokyo Institute of Arts, and cast in copper, then overlaid with gold.

The guinea pig is still in Ibuka's office—and it remains a potent symbol of his devotion to a gutsy ideal.

From the first days in the small rooms on the third and seventh floors of the Shirokiya department store, Masaru Ibuka had been devoted to the unique—and also to quality. Though Sony has continued to provide products for commercial use, the main thrust of its research and development has always been consumer items. Ibuka built this concept into the prospectus for Tokyo Telecommunications, and embodied it even in his early development of the ill-fated rice cooker. He is a trailblazer with the temperament of a dedicated research scientist, and he couples this with a firm commitment to the practical application of this science. Beyond all that, he has the one infallible mark of genius: the ability to think of something that has not been known before, to break the walls of existing theory.

Ibuka has always had an intense interest in toys and puzzles, and on each of his many trips abroad has managed to return with several new items. In such toys he says he finds the "seeds" for new products.

Seeds. The word is an exceptionally important one at Sony. I heard it repeatedly—in English, for there is no significant Japanese equivalent—from the chief engineers and from the director of research.

Nobutoshi Kihara, a mechanical engineer who joined the firm after graduating from college in 1947, has worked most closely with Ibuka over the years, and is centrally responsible for many of Sony's most famous products. In the forties he developed the magnetic paper tape used on the first tape recorders, and the carbon microphone with loudspeaker used to create a resonating circuit; he created the AC bias recording system and worked closely on the radio and television units used with the first transistor devices; he was the first to transistorize the tape recorder, and has been responsible for scores of pioneering developments connected to the use of first audio and then video tape recording. In the early days, before the semiconductor and color television divisions became separate, before a separate research center was founded, Kihara was in charge of all developmental work. He is a tall, quiet, scholarly man—with dreamy eyes, a soft handshake, and a love of golf.

In the forties and fifties Ibuka would come to him, he says, "with the seed or hint of an idea" and ask him to try it out. Kihara would then work on the project and return to Ibuka with his results. "But when we came up with solutions," Kihara says, "and though this pointed to a good product, top management inevitably came back with a different demand. They would say, 'Well, that sort of product is something

A product development office, c. 1956. Kihara, who has been responsible for so many new products at Sony, is in the center foreground.

anyone can develop. It is not sufficiently different—or important.'" Then Ibuka would ask Kihara and his team to shift the elements so that the product would become *uniquely* useful. Sometimes the demands would radically shift the original direction of development, sometimes only modifications were asked for. "But the challenge was always there," Kihara says, and this spurred them on.

This process is a central one at Sony; it is coupled with the expert establishment of a "target."

Target. Another word I heard repeated over and over—in English—in the research, development, and production engineering divisions.

Ibuka admits that it is a general characteristic of Japanese industry to wait until a discovery is deemed feasible and then to "jump at it and be very quick and efficient in producing a modified version. In Japanese technology engineers don't have to know the details—only that something is possible." Such outside stimulation is actually one of the greatest spurs to all industrial creativity today. Sony, of course, has usually been an exception, a "guinea pig," but it has not been totally free of this general Japanese trait—nor, necessarily, does it want to. "As soon as we heard the news that Ampex had developed the first VTR," Ibuka says, "our development staff, headed by Kihara then, began working on the concept. Three months later we made our first successful video tape recorder—which shows the importance of proper leadership and guidance, of having the proper target in technical development."

Later VTR development shows even more clearly this targeting process at Sony, combined with its special focus on the new and the most useful. The first VTR system Kihara created in the early 1950s was quite similar to the Ampex system (and as one engineer said, "It was as heavy as an anchor"). Kihara thought it would be a great source of business even though it would have to sell for 20 million yen. But Ibuka insisted: "We are not going to make broadcast equipment; we want to make home video. If you can make one like this, you can also

make one for home use. Develop one that will sell in the range
of 2 million yen."

Kihara did so, and was soon told: "Now make one that will
sell for 200,000 yen."

Thus, after the U-Matic video cassette had been developed
and marketed successfully for commercial use, the next step
was a small, less expensive unit for home use. Ibuka not only
provided the expected price but actually specified the size he
wanted. "He gave us the actual target and the dimensions of
the target," says Kihara, "and we knew we had the technology
to achieve this."

Actually, there were ten different ways of possibly achiev-
ing the desired result; each had to be tried to see which was
most feasible. Kihara mobilized his entire division and they
began at once to test out their various options, with each of
several groups—in parallel efforts—trying out a different system.
After about eighteen months of developmental work, they selected the unit they wanted to perfect; then they began another
eighteen months of work with the production engineers. In
May 1975, Sony announced the Betamax home video tape recording unit.

Sony's exceptionally broad technological base made the
Betamax possible; the unit required expertise in a dozen
areas Sony had pioneered since the late 1940s. Such a broad
range of interests also made possible Esaki's discovery of the
"tunneling effect"—for only Sony was working toward achievement of the best performance of what was called the PN junction transistor at the time. And such breadth will provide immense support for the future; as Morita says, "as the speed of
technological innovation accelerates, the importance of research
and development becomes even greater."

To ensure flexibility in this high-pressured developmental
stage, Kihara's division keeps expanding and contracting, depending upon whether they are in an experimental or production development stage; a whole group of his people followed
the pilot Betamax into the production engineering department.

He normally has 120 workers in his division and there are another 200 in other engineering development sections; in all, there are about 800 employees at Sony engaged in research and development work.

Dr. Makoto Kikuchi, the current director of research, emphatically stresses Sony's concern for targeting in his division, too. Though it is widely rumored that Sony spends a vastly greater proportion of gross sales on research than other firms, Kikuchi says this is simply not so. He insists that Sony's slogan, "Research makes the difference," is an operating force—but that the difference does not exist in the "level of technology" or "the quality of the engineers" or even in the amount of money budgeted for development, about 5 percent of gross sales, which *is* rather high. The main difference lies in "the control of engineering power, the establishment of mission-oriented research and proper targets."

Targets.

"Many other companies give their researchers *full* freedom," says Kikuchi. "We find a strategy, an aim, a very real and clear *target* and then establish the necessary task forces to get the job done."

Here too much of the impetus comes from Ibuka, who gets his original hints by what one colleague called "swift animal intuition," then has the brilliance to plant the proper seeds, then the foresight (with Morita) to see the best possible use for a scientific development in the consumer sphere. Often an idea is debunked vigorously—discussed, argued, analyzed, and perhaps dropped; but once the commitment to go ahead is made, says Kikuchi, "once Ibuka focuses his interest, he *never* gives up."

Ibuka's spirit pervades all the research and development work at Sony, where he has created a truly open relationship that defies the bureaucracy Kikuchi fought for twenty-six years at MITI and which exists in most other Japanese manufacturing firms. Ibuka likes to "sit and let people talk; that's where good ideas come from." He still goes frequently to the laboratories in his blue work jacket, talks with the men, encourages that requisite independence, and continues to evaluate the practical promise of new innovations and establish new directions. He has a decisive and long-range sense of priorities. When Kikuchi came to one of the regular Tuesday morning meetings of the executive committee not long ago with a request for a new systems machine for higher precision work in semiconductor research, Ibuka asked only why it was needed and how much it would cost. He at once saw the importance of the machine and persuaded the committee (most of whom, uniquely, are scientists) to import one from America as soon as possible. Its cost was 100 million yen, about $330,000. "We don't spare money for fundamental research," says Ibuka. "Progress itself reinforces the company's energy, which is indispensable for success."

The first separate research laboratory at Sony was founded in June 1961 under the directorship of Dr. G. M. Hatoyama (the current president of the North Shore College). Its function was "to provide the scientific foundation of basic and applied research for future Sony products." The laboratory was reorganized in 1969, absorbing and consolidating the research staff from all divisions, and housed in a large new facility in Yokohama. Today, with more than two hundred staff members, special departments have been created for material research, semiconductor research, information processing, and material analysis.

With this wide spectrum of activities, the Research Center strives to correlate all projects with practical problems. Kikuchi says that "need" and "seed" form the basis for most of the center's activities. Sometimes they will be brought a "problem looking for a solution"; some shorting of the electric circuit on television sets was discovered, brought to their attention, and the difficulty established. When they opened the tin can covering the electric resistor to protect it from moisture, they found a very thin wire, like a cat's whisker, growing from the metal surface and causing the shorting effect. No one knew how

The Sony Research Center in Yokohama.

it was formed, so they first analyzed the material of this growth, determined that it was caused by high temperatures, and developed a method of preventing its recurrence.

Much work today focuses on improving the fundamental characteristics of basic products in an effort to effect better performance.

Laboratory technicians continue to study such Sony mainstays as magnetic tape, trying to distribute the magnetic particles (which want to congregate in groups) more uniformly so that performance will be better; they strive to increase the capacity of the tapes to take a higher density of information. In the semiconductor field, though there has been a marked maturing of the technology and fewer startling innovations are expected—in the past twenty-five years most of the physical phenomena have been observed—the center developed only last year the SIPOS, a new transistor device that is smaller, more reliable, and easier to produce. Though the probability of discovering the new continues to decrease, and Ibuka knows this, he says: "We must not forget, however, that the probability of *missing* a promising seed is also high"—so they must play strenuously against the wheel.

Research and development in color television continues, and has led to an improved Trinitron with 60 percent more picture brightness; during the energy crisis, it led to the Econoquick device, which allows the picture to appear without preheating, five seconds after the switch is thrown. In this field, where competition is severe, Sony (like many other companies) is constantly seeking improvement and development of basic performance and what are called "charming features of practical value." Someone in America, where Kikuchi often travels (he once taught at MIT and is a close friend of William Shockley, who invented the transistor for Bell Laboratories), asked him to develop a set that "automatically shuts down at commercials."

The maturing of the technology is coupled with what may be an even more interesting phenomenon—what I would call a "maturing of interest in the new." We have seen, in the past thirty years, extraordinary harnessing of technology for consumer use. Are consumers now bored or even burdened by this —with its attendant instant obsolescence? When I proudly showed my new Sony tape recorder to a shrewd and experienced editor of *Television Digest,* he grumbled: "By the end of the year they will have one smaller, with better and smaller tape." I rather like my new tape recorder; I would rather like to live with it for a half dozen years without worrying that I am missing out on something better. It took me a long time to acquire this one and I have very little personal need for many other electronics products. Kobo Abe, the Japanese novelist, speaks of each individual in modern times as "hopelessly inundated by change." I resist it. Apparently I am not alone. When Kikuchi recently asked Dr. Shockley what would or should come after color television, Shockley sheepishly admitted that he still hadn't bought a color set. Pressed further, he showed Kikuchi his old black-and-white console; it was so old that pliers are needed to work the switches.

Still, Sony has depended from its origin on the new and is constantly experimenting within its range of interests. At the higher price brackets, they have developed in recent years a huge 10-foot-screen projector television that sells for a cozy $23,000 and a replete Golf Clinic System that you can ask your local sports center to buy for $35,000. This clinic is a remarkable contraption, a marvel to behold. Among its twenty-two separate features are: balance and speed sensor boards, a front-view fixed video camera, a mobile video camera, a speed sensor lamp, a balance checker a speed checker, a sheet video-corder, two remote control panels, a 20-inch special double monitor television, and an external monitor television. And what can such an elaborate system do? Well, in time periods of several tenths of a second, it can analyze high-speed actions such as the locus and movement of a golf club. It can measure the exact shift and movement of a golfer's weight between his left and right feet during the swing. And it can simultaneously measure the movement of such objects as the club's head during the swing and the ball's initial velocity after it has been hit. Since every picture frame can be played back any number of times, the golfer can isolate his problem and, perhaps, cure it— the system cannot do the latter. While I visited one of the laboratories, I saw Fusako Masui, a professional golfer, having her swing checked, her stroke analyzed through slow-motion playback, by a tall, austere, white-haired professor of sports psychology, Tetsuo Ohta. Japanese take their golf seriously. They even write haiku about it.

Heitaro Nakajima, who spent twenty-three years in the research and development division of NHK, now heads the audio division at Sony. With 43 percent of its total sales generated in this field, audio remains extremely important. Nakajima reaffirmed the very advanced technology Sony had in solid state and magnetics, and the constant need to improve

The 120-inch screen color video projection system.

quality and content. Eighty to 90 percent of Sony's new ideas in audio derive from his division—with the others coming from experiments in other divisions and from market research. Top managers from all the major research or development divisions meet regularly to share new developments, get valuable feedback, and consider possible new projects. Nakajima stressed that not only does Ibuka constantly support and encourage development but that Morita does so as well, with practical suggestions that demonstrate—even after all his years heading the marketing and financial areas—he has not forgotten his early training in physics.

Morita, in his brilliant Frank Nelson Doubleday lecture, "Creativity in Modern Industry," stresses the difference between the days of Leonardo or Newton or Edison, when a single genius could create a major innovation, and today, when most significant advances require a broad coordination of many different technologies. Certainly there must be an environment that inspires creativity but there must also be yoking of disparate specialties. It becomes the function of management, he says, "to bring into collaboration many persons," mobilizing the entire engineering capacity of the firm, drawing upon every available source in an extraordinarily "information-rich" society. Communication within the firm, the establishment of living arteries to share available skills, is absolutely necessary to bring new ideas to fruition. And then, there must be further coordination of the production technology and eventually the marketing, if the product is to be produced with quality control and reliable budgeting, and then sell enough units to remain viable. He spotlights Ibuka's constant presence during the development of the Trinitron as exceptionally rare and important: Top management could thereby coordinate, decide on personnel and funding priorities quickly, and implement decisions with otherwise impossible speed.

There is an electronics product for even the most skeptical. That irresistible little pocket tape recorder I acquired in Tokyo, the TC-1100 Cassette-corder, is both elegant and highly efficient. Nakajima told me he had taken a full two years to develop it.

How could they obtain such exceptional quality?

Nakajima said there was constant interchange between the designing staff and the production line; if any error occurred in the production process, the item immediately went back for further design work. Parts had to be of excellent quality, and Sony maintained extremely strict and rigid reliability tests. There were drop tests; mechanical shock tests, in which the equipment was packed in a container, then rotated severely in a hexagonal drum; and environment tests. "If most manufacturers test a product in control rooms —5° C. to 50° C.," he told me, "we will stretch that to —20° to 60° C. It is the same for humidity and other tests. We are stringent. We go beyond what the others do."

The newest development in the audio division is a 300-watt audio amplifier—small, flatter, and incorporating a new "pulse with amplification" (PWA) system. It has not yet been marketed. Since the product is machined out of a solid piece of aluminum, it has no joints; it weighs only twelve pounds, rather than the seventy-five pounds an amplifier with its power would usually have to weigh. It is silver gray, rectangular, and to me looked for all the world like a sleek box from a chic Madison Avenue boutique.

One of the greatest disappointments to Kihara and other men in developmental work is—quite naturally—to produce a viable product and then not see it marketed. Kihara remembers when Ibuka in the early 1950s first saw a stereophonic recorder in America, he telegraphed full details back to Tokyo. Kihara had created a two-track system by the time Ibuka returned, and had brought in musicians and made a live recording for him. Ibuka was delighted. He thought the marketing prospects were excellent.

But the market wasn't ready. In 1955 Sony dropped their

stereo development—only to see it succeed for Japan Victor some years later; when Sony finally entered the stereo market, they were late.

They developed a transistorized clock—and then sold the patent to Seiko.

They developed the first electronic desk calculator in the world—and, in a special presentation, gave the Smithsonian Institution one of the first units, to go with earlier presentations of Sony's transistor radio and its world's first all-transistor black-and-white television. Then, when top management saw the handwriting on the wall, it dropped the product. Many salesmen and engineers were highly disappointed at this, especially since the division was in the black, but the hard decision was unquestionably sound.

Though some of these dropped projects cost the firm hundreds of thousands of dollars—and may properly be considered failures—this kind of flexibility is characteristic of Sony. The company constantly reevaluates its research targets and marketing capabilities. Peter Drucker says that top management must persistently ask: "What is our business? What *will* our business be?" Sony not only does this but has built into its operative structure the mechanics for rapid change. It constantly reassesses its engineering capacity, too: Rather than devote too much time and staff to a product it finally deems minor, it will

Sony's SOBAX ICC-600W electronic calculator, introduced in America in October 1968.

This Mavica system was shown at the International Magnetic Conference held in Toronto in May 1974. The Mavica has not yet been marketed. A new model, with improvements, is now ready but has not been publicly announced.

shift back to its fundamental strengths and reaffirm its commitment to "narrow but deep" specialization.

Sony has an electronic organ it has not commercialized—fitted with a recording unit so one could play a duet with oneself if one was so disposed. It also developed the Mavica Magnetic Video-Card System and actually introduced this in Montreal in 1974. A magnetic card can be inserted into the machine, which records and plays back the picture and sound in normal motion, slow, still, or reverse. They still haven't decided how —or if—to market this. And they have various video games that flash a picture on the television screen and provide buttons for indicating your answers to such questions as "Excluding the claws, how many legs has a crab? Four legs? Six legs? Eight legs? Ten legs? Please make your choice." I did, and was usually wrong—but this does not prevent me from thinking the item cleverly made but silly. Morita apparently agrees; at a recent meeting with security analysts in New York he laughed lightly when these games were mentioned, and said Sony has no immediate plans to market them.

I'm glad.

I didn't much like an experimental children's toy, either, which provided a flash card fitted with prerecorded tape that, when inserted, boomed, "Humpty-Dumpty sat on a . . ." I kept wondering if Ibuka would really have become Ibuka if he had been subjected to such toys when he was a boy—or learned his science from Sony's "Audiovisual Learning Laboratory." There are educators—a great number of them—who like such educational aides. I'm not one of them. They seem to me to *remove* the thing to be learned rather than drawing it closer. We learn one on one—with the thing itself.

The range of new consumer products actually being marketed is impressive. There are various new and smaller tape recorders and dictating machines (Sony will soon expand its business machines marketing); radio clocks in a broad variety of handsome models; integrated component music systems; hi-fidelity components; a new wide-angle television tube with a 114° rather than 110° angle; and the new Trinitron, with a picture 60 percent brighter. For commercial use, there is an impressive electronic editing machine. Though Sony has a CB radio, it has not committed itself strongly to this product. Morita announced in February 1976 his doubts about Sony's interest in CB—though the market is ballooning wildly in America today.

Dr. Kikuchi, an exceptionally open and intensely curious man, constantly asks visitors and perfect strangers for "seeds." I allowed that I would like to see longer playing time on the cassettes used with my new tape recorder, and batteries that would run for much longer periods of time. Technically, they are able to increase the playing time by slowing down the tape

Top left, a Sony digital clock radio, model TFM-C770. *Top right,* the BM-11 portable dictating machine. The unit uses standard cassettes. *Center left,* a Sony clock radio. *Bottom right,* in 1972 Sony first marketed this receiver for 4-channel and stereo with two built-in decoding circuits.

Above, the new Cassette-corder. *Right,* Sony's 32-band "world zone" portable radio.

Center left, this compact stereo music system with cassette tape recorder was introduced in America in April 1976. The suggested retail price is $350. *Center right,* this three-band radio, introduced in 1976, folds into a hand-held unit. *Bottom left,* Sony has always produced a few really oddball items such as this 1970 AM radio.

speed, he explained at once, or producing thinner tape (though Philips maintains strict control over all manufacturers on standard audio cassette tape speed at present); the duration of batteries might well be increased.

More fascinating than my suggestions are projects under way to develop special memory devices connected to the use of the transistor, and experiments with the use of light (which behaves like a carrier) for information processing and communication. Sony, like many other companies throughout the world, would like to produce a low-cost color video camera, perhaps one that could make cassettes for use with its Betamax —but this seems a long way down the road. It is attempting to apply electronics to the problems of color printing, which would be an exciting development. And it is well along in the development of a flat-panel television, which will hang on a wall and make the picture tube obsolete.

What will be next?

What major new product is in the offing?

When Kihara looks back, he notes that it was often impossible to predict then how far a particular technology could be developed. He could not do so now.

"But aren't there specific new products, major innovations, that you are working on now?" I ask.

His calm face brightens slyly and he says, in English, "Secret."

With his record, that's a pregnant word.

CHAPTER TEN

Multi- or
Internationatism

*For business purposes, the boundaries that separate
one nation from another are no more real than
the equator.*

—JACQUES G. MAISONROUGE

*To multinationals, the whole world has become
one global shopping center.*

—PETER F. DRUCKER

*The multinational corporation, which combines
modern management with liberal trade policies,
is arguably the most creative institution of the
twentieth century.*

—DANIEL P. MOYNIHAN

UNTIL THE late 1950s, Sony was a domestic company, gen-
erating the major portion of its sales in Japan; the sixties
were characterized by its dramatic move into the export market,
and it then established scores of distributorships and wholly

166

owned subsidiaries throughout the world that functioned under tight Tokyo control. But for twenty years Morita had been thinking increasingly in global terms. In the seventies Sony entered into a number of exciting joint ventures, became an importer of foreign goods, placed top nationals in charge of many of its foreign subsidiaries, established its first offshore production facilities, and became a truly international company. (Morita avoids, "because of bad connotations," the word "multinational.") This was, in Drucker's phrase, "a normal, indeed a necessary, response to economic reality."

As early as 1962, before Morita lived in New York, he contemplated the construction of a Sony plant in America; another Japanese company had decided to build their own factory here, and the idea was intriguing. But Morita thought it was too early: Wages in Japan were rising but still modest in comparison to American salaries; freight was not prohibitive; but chiefly, Sony did not yet have the sales capability to warrant such a venture—they had not yet created a sufficient market. The other company believed they should build their factory first, then establish their market. It didn't work—and the factory failed.

The enormous success of the Trinitron in the late 1960s gave American sales a tremendous boost. The sales network that Ray Steiner had consolidated now fully proved its worth.

Sonam had come to a point where it had to expand more, and at the same time the tremendous influx of Japanese products into the United States (and severe import regulations by the Japanese government) had created an imbalance of trade that could cause serious problems for Sony. Morita and Iwama (who served as president of Sonam in the early 1970s) foresaw the dangers to come—and they came fast and hard. Strong anti-Japanese sentiment brought about charges of dumping in 1970, a decision that included Sony—though in December 1970, the United States Treasury Department exonerated the company, and continuing review reaffirmed this in February 1975. Then, in the summer of 1971, in what became known as the "Nixon

Shock," the American President imposed economic controls that dictated a price freeze, a surcharge on imports, and an end to the convertibility of the dollar into gold. Between December 1971 and February 1973, the yen was sharply revalued, from 360 to the dollar to 265.

Morita began an intensive "Americanization" program. Ira Morais says he would call at four or five in the morning (saying, "Anyone who works for Sony doesn't sleep!") and suggest ways of furthering Sony's image. Within a short time he had two major thrusts: Americans owned stock in Sony and Americans worked in Sony's San Diego plant. There were other telling changes as well.

In 1970 Sony became the first Japanese company to list its stocks for trading on the New York Stock Exchange. Ever since its American Depositary Receipts (ADRs) were traded

Sony products head across the Pacific by a chartered jet.

On September 17, 1970, Sony became the first Japanese firm to be listed on the New York Stock Exchange. *From left to right:* Akio Morita, Robert Haack (president of the New York Stock Exchange), and Noboru Yoshii check the ticker tape for SNE. *Photo by Paul Schumach*

over the counter in 1961, the stock had been highly volatile. With the success of the Trinitron, and listing on the big board, interest in Sony, now assigned ticker symbol SNE, broadened considerably. More and more institutions began to carry it in their portfolios: It became, for many brokerage houses, not "an interesting new company, perhaps too erratic," but a solid growth stock, supported by the company's "vast technology, able management, and aggressive marketing." Sony now has over 100 institutional holders, substantially fewer than Kodak's 720 or IBM's 1,200 (companies Morita especially admires) but interest continues to increase.

Opinions vary sharply, in good part due to the difficulty many American observers have in understanding Japanese economics. One analyst, pointing to Sony's debt-to-short-term-equity ratio, called the company "financially obscene." I have seen absolutely no evidence of this. The availability of short-term money has been the bulwark of Japanese industry for the past thirty years, and the country averages are almost opposite those that exist in American firms. Drucker says that 70 percent debt capital and 30 percent equity capital are the norm in Japan (where there is no long-term debt market, and a company's relations with its bank are so close that virtually never would "the plug be pulled") and exactly the opposite in America; but I have seen numerous estimations that Japan's average debt-to-equity ratio is as low as 75 to 25 percent. Robert Czepiel, research vice-president at Cyrus J. Lawrence and a "specialist" at Sony stock, notes that Sony's 40 to 45 percent equity capital is exceedingly rare for a Japanese company and that "its ratios keep getting better." To further consolidate its financial attractiveness to American investors, Sony got an AA Standard & Poor rating when it floated bonds to raise capital for the new Dothan, Alabama, tape plant it is building.

Top management has for years been pioneering (for a Japanese company) the acquisition of capital through shares. This began in 1950, when Tokyo Telecommunications first offered its stock (as an actual substitute for the difficulty it had, as a small new firm, acquiring expansion money); the principal had been advanced by Yoshii, a peppery, bouncy man who came to Sony from the Mitsui Bank. Yoshii has gotten Sony listed on fifteen major stock exchanges throughout the world, and sharply reduced its short-term money in recent years. He and Sumio Sano, the financial relations manager at Sonam, spend considerable time every year, traveling across America and talking with groups of potential investors, trying to make the complicated Japanese balance sheet less opaque. Sony's stronger ratios are helping considerably. "They're building a *bank*," says Czepiel. And to this might be added the fact that for years Morita and Ibuka have spoken of building a *bank* of knowledge and technology—which are now available both for their own production needs and as a viable inducement to companies looking for joint-venture or royalty-free cross-licensing agreements.

Sony's major joint-venture agreement with CBS in 1966 has been enormously successful. It grossed $4 million in its first six months; this year sales topped $80 million, with a $15 million pretax profit. More joint-ventures and cross-licensing agreements have followed, knitting Sony closer to America and Europe. Rosiny, who negotiated the major North American ventures, says: "Because Sony's reputation in industry is so excellent, even though the company is relatively small, negotiations were invariably cordial, eyeball to eyeball." Sony established an important 50-50 joint-venture agreement with Texas Instruments in Japan, which enabled the American company (long kept out because MITI wouldn't permit 100 percent foreign-owned firms in) to enter the Japanese market; Sony has since sold back its 50 percent share. As early as 1965, IBM sought out Sony guidance and help in developing its own magnetic tape production. "In the phenomenally short period between December 1965 and July 1966," says J. W. Birkenstock, formerly of IBM, "Sony built us a plant in Japan, flew it over, and installed it in Boulder, Colorado. In October 1967 we put our product on the market, in about half the time we normally allow for such a program." Most recently, Sony entered into a joint-venture agreement with Union Carbide to market Sony-Eveready batteries in Japan.

Morita further decided to counter the severe imbalance of trade by boldly establishing the Sony Trading Corporation. "Sony Wants to Sell U.S. Products in Japan" ran the headline of a full-page advertisement in *Time* and other leading magazines and newspapers in mid-1971; similar ads followed in England, France, Italy, and West Germany. By July 1972, Sony was in the import business, another pioneering gesture, using its marketing expertise in Japan to create a strong, profitable new venture that would counter the increasing wave of Japanese imports. Sony brought in and successfully marketed Schick electric razors, towels, kitchenware, Thorne gas heaters, Regalware pots and pans, Branzeer kitchen units, Heathkit products, Whirlpool washers—products mass-produced in America, England, and the Netherlands. It was a unique switch, and has recently included even the purchase of rights by Sony Enterprises to N.F.L. football emblems and films, which has helped to produce a major (and highly lucrative) fad, the current craze in Japan for American football emblems on shoes, socks, posters, and even school notebooks.

From its inception in February 1960 until January 1966, Morita served as president of Sonam. However, except for the time Morita lived in the United States, the actual operational head of the subsidiary was Shigeru Inagaki, its executive vice-president. In 1966 Ernest Schwarzenbach (a retired executive of Smith Barney, the company that had been managing underwriter of Sony's ADR public offering in 1961) succeeded Morita as president of Sonam and functioned in that capacity until his death in September 1968. Then Morita again became president of Sonam, though up to May 1971 it was managed by an executive committee chaired by Rosiny. From May 1971 until September 1972, Iwama lived in America and served as president of Sonam. His successor was Harvey Schein, a forty-four-year-old former president of CBS International. Schein's appointment was ample evidence that Morita was ready to delegate preponderant responsibility to a young, vigorous American president.

Some Sonam employees found Schein "too tight" at first, but he has tried to change his style. "I'm becoming more and more Japanese in the way I do business," he says. He has lunch with middle management once a week and has adopted a modified consensus system of decision-making. He speaks with pleasure of helping the young Japanese managers Morita sends over "to be trained into truly international-thinking executives" and of the Japanese employee who asked him for the name of a good English teacher—which Schein got him, and also arranged lessons. He notes ruefully that he was at CBS for fourteen years and didn't see Paley or Stanton until he had become a top executive of CBS, and wonders what their reaction would have been had he asked them to find him, say, a Spanish teacher.

Iwama had earlier recognized that there was an even more important gesture needed: Sony *must* now manufacture in the United States using American workers. He told Morita, who readily agreed.

When Morita announced his decision to build a Sony plant some twenty miles north of San Diego, the American press noted that all the *American* companies were going East, to Taiwan and Singapore. Morita said wryly: "I always go in the opposite direction."

Iwama speaks to local dignitaries and employees at the groundbreaking ceremony for Sony's San Diego plant.

The American media have tried to lump what Sony has done in San Diego under the general umbrella, "Japanese Management in the United States." There are indeed some characteristics in common, whether the firm is producing zippers, bearings, textiles, soy sauce, or Trinitrons. There is, as Louis Kraar noted in a recent *Fortune* article, a common "yen for harmony": Japanese managers all seek to avoid major confrontations, to promote internal peace; they encourage far more discussions and meetings than an American firm, and attempt to adopt the traditional consensus method of decision-making at all levels; they try to create something approaching a family atmosphere.

But these general characteristics are most distinguishing relative to American management practices. "Before anything else they see us as Japanese," insists Mike Morimoto, the vigorous, outspoken young assistant general manager at the San Diego plant; he has a law degree from prestigious Tokyo University, spent a year in Columbia graduate school, and reads Henry Miller and Anaïs Nin. "But I think that is a bunch of balonies. We are not a Japanese but an international company; *Sony* concepts are the constant factor."

Morimoto, along with Steve Kodera, the first Japanese manager of the San Diego plant (who was recently replaced by Shiro Yamada, former general manager of the Inazawa plant), and an American, Ron Dishno, were there from the start. Before the $25 million plant was completed in July 1972 on a pleasant hill in the Rancho Bernardo Industrial Park, they were working together, building a staff, ordering supplies, and developing their own management policies. Iwama had only told Morimoto: "Don't make it look like a plant!" And they had arranged to have bright yellow, red, and blue designs painted on the walls of the spacious, airy building.

Dishno, a tall, lean young man who had majored in economics at college, had no experience in television assembly; he had spent ten years working for an American electronics component manufacturer. He thought Sony would bring in a lot of its own people and have preconceived ideas on management policy. He was pleasantly surprised that this was not the case. Japanese engineers, some twenty of them, came over to establish the plant technology, which follows that in the Osaki and Ichinomiya plants closely, and definite production goals and standards were established: Beyond that, the new managers were given such a free hand that both Dishno and Morimoto felt they were truly pioneering, with all the excitement and energy the word implies; today they feel they have been running their own business for the past four years, "without the financial worries."

"I thought there would be ironclad rules," says Dishno, "but within broad guidelines, they not only let but actually encouraged us to formulate our own employment practices, personnel and many manufacturing policies, and most else." The managers were all in their early thirties and rose to what Dishno calls "the opportunity of a lifetime." Iwama came over frequently and encouraged them to talk freely with him. "We saw he liked and respected us," says Dishno, "and with his character and charisma, and the trust with which he gave us freedom, we worked like demons." Whenever necessary, they put in twenty-hour days.

The San Diego plant began with a bare thirty employees, and responsibility only for assembling Trinitrons from parts shipped from Japan. But they soon added actual tube production, began to assemble some audio equipment, and started to purchase most of their components from carefully selected American manufacturers. The number of employees grew rapidly to several hundred, then 1,000; eventually the number will be increased to about 1,300, perhaps maximum for such a plant in Sony's view.

Since there were few major electronics companies manufacturing in the San Diego area, there was no available pool of experienced workers, as would have been the case had Sony decided to assemble and manufacture in Pennsylvania or various sections in the Midwest. This proved a distinct advantage.

Sony likes to train its workers from scratch, its own way. Morimoto says that, since most workers enter unskilled, they basically looked for the proper attitude. "We spend a lot of time interviewing," he says. "Before we hire anyone, they have had three separate interviews. A new worker must like the kind of work she will be doing and be eager to do a good job." Dishno adds that the individual section supervisors with whom the prospective employee will work undertake the last interview. "They make the final selection," he says, "and since they have hired their own people and are able to handpick those they will need to meet their production schedules, they won't have any excuses!" Once he has hired someone, a supervisor will spend at least an hour with the new worker, outlining Sony's history and reputation for quality, and its local management policies. During the actual training period, supervisors not only attempt to develop good assembly techniques, an enthusiasm for work, and a commitment to quality, but also a sense of how much the final product depends upon each individual employee; even a small mistake can affect the entire line, and potentially mar the performance of a set. Each worker is not a cog but a valuable member of the team. Some workers are eventually cross-trained, learning several or more of the different stations in the line—so they will see the entire process and, if they prefer, be able to avoid the monotony of doing only one job; some actually prefer to do only one job.

Most supervisors are promoted from the assembly line and thus know not only the general principles of television production but Sony's exact method. The company sponsors special engineering classes, held at the plant and tailored to Sony's specific needs.

Perhaps the greatest single challenge to the American managers were the seemingly endless meetings. The Americans often preferred to make decisions themselves, without so much talking—they thought discussions were a waste of time; and some of the Japanese seemed, to the Americans, to want to talk endlessly, to avoid any final confrontations whereby one or the other might lose face. Morimoto, who separates himself boldly from traditional Japanese methods—in fact, dislikes the overbearing qualities of *amae*—says: "The purpose of the meetings is primarily to assure that all people have the same quantity and quality of information. Objectively, the problem may be composed of elements A, B, C, D, and E, but some people only know A and C and think they know it all, and others only know B and D, or just E. We want everyone to start with all the facts. Consensus takes time but it *is* important; one person may have to make the final decision, because a plant cannot be a purely democratic structure, but it is valuable for management to act as one unit. Too often in Japan, just reaching a consensus—so no one will lose face—becomes the objective," which is also "a bunch of balonies."

Dishno himself found it hard at first to adjust to the large number of meetings. "We seemed to be spending an inordinate amount of time on those small problems," he says. "But I saw that by getting as many people involved as possible, when you reach a decision you have far less resistance to contend with. Implementation is swift. Everyone understands and by this time supports the final plan. Frankly, I would find it difficult to return to a system where authoritarian decisions merely come down from the top."

San Diego also tried to eliminate any direct chain-of-command or organizational chart form of structure. "We involve various people, as needed for a problem, in a task-force approach," Dishno says, "drawing them from various parts of the firm because of their special skill, experience, and knowledge. Most of these people normally would have no direct responsibility and the decision would be made only by one person who was in charge of that function—but who might not know all the implications."

At first, all frontline supervisors met with the workers on their line once a day; but they didn't have enough to say to each other, so this was changed to once or twice a week. Once a month there was also a general meeting of the thirty-five to forty supervisors. Working within the broad parameters of cost, quality, and quantity—establishing their own budget rather than having an industrial engineering department direct them —many of these supervisors consider their units as their own little companies. They hire their own workers, train and cross-train them, teach, promote, motivate, and shift them according to their own best judgment.

"It is not a Japanese but a Sony philosophy to give autonomy to middle managers," says Dishno. "It is unique with Sony that top management does not direct so much as advise." All managers try to be available, under the open-door policy, to the supervisors and even line workers. "This takes a tremendous amount of effort, there are tons of details, but it is worth everything," says Dishno. In Kobayashi's terms—and you can see much of his concern for human beings throughout this plant, though modified and adjusted—this eliminates the small-pebble complex and increases connection.

In 1972, right after the plant opened, the workers were handbilled by a local union, then approached again a short time later. In 1974 the union had made sufficient inroads to demand a vote. This represented a major challenge to the new plant. Though Morimoto recognized "the historical basis for unions," he was genuinely concerned that, in this case, they would be counterproductive, slowing down plant processes, creating automatic benefits rather than organic changes; he also felt that those pressing for unionization were a "loud minority" rather than a true representation of plant sentiment.

He secured all possible information on the Communications Workers Union, studied its local and international bylaws, retained a local labor-relations lawyer to check relevant court cases. In many instances, he felt some of the union benefits had been exaggerated by the organizers; in some court cases it seemed apparent to him that the union had not acted for bottom-line rank and file.

Chiefly, though, Morimoto wanted to inform the workers exactly where they stood. He and Dishno began a series of small meetings—arranging to meet every member of the plant staff personally, in groups of up to twelve. They explained that Sony's base pay was on the high end of local scales; that the vacation, sick leave, profit-sharing, and pension-plan programs compared favorably with those the union advocated, and, interestingly, were in some cases *higher* than those the union promised. The two young men wanted most to reinforce the human connection between management and labor, to stress that they were both engaged, for the benefit of all, in maintaining high quality and high reliability; that the environment in which they all worked was of constant concern to management. They reminded the workers of the open-door policy that characterized Sony management, how *all* the frontline supervisors had been promoted from within, and how they had avoided any layoffs even at times of exceptional stress. (Once, in 1973, when the plant had trouble getting the proper cabinets from Los Angeles vendors, the workers, terrified that there would be a layoff, began to check the cabinet inventory daily—but Dishno and Morimoto assured them they would not be laid off.)

To facilitate communication between line workers and management, they instituted an "Action Line" telephone (to replace the infrequently used suggestion boxes); from any corner of the plant a worker could dial 300 and either a manager would answer the question or it would be tape-recorded and answered within twenty-four hours. The snack bar was promptly cleaned, when this was requested, and more pay telephones added; but Morimoto says that "the best thing was that we all got to know each other better." The plant now also publishes a four-page monthly newssheet, *Sony NewsBoy*, a lively little paper with practical information about such matters as holidays, special events, promotions, and a host of personal items; an "Action Line 300" column publically answers some of the more interesting questions that have come in by phone.

Unlike the practice in Sony's Japan-based plants, all promotions on the assembly line in San Diego were at first based on merit; those trying to organize the union wanted it partially based on merit, partially on seniority—and management agreed to this. The organizers felt that management's calls for overtime, to meet necessary production goals, were too abrupt; management and labor agreed that two days' notice would be fair, and that management need only expect 70 percent of those called to agree to work overtime.

Several news and magazine articles have implied that Sony was gilding the lily, bending over backward to soothe labor with candy; this appears not to be the case. They gave understanding; they provided communication; they listened.

Dishno and Morimoto both think that the vote would have gone the same way had they not talked so much to the workers—that the vote was really a confirmation of the initial and healthy policies San Diego had established. Plant workers voted 299 to 100 against unionization, nearly three to one.

Are there still problems in San Diego?

No plant this size is free from problems. Personnel and management policies undergo constant review; communication is, everywhere, a daily challenge. What is the best format for work evaluations? How often should they be made? How can budget be met in a given season?

Though most of the managers today are American, there are still some misunderstandings. Many Japanese, Morimoto says, still have to learn to say, "I don't understand the question." (Top management at Sony, for all its marvelous independence, still often say "I see" when they are asked a poorly phrased question in English.) And many Americans still grow frustrated, he says, because some Japanese managers do not clearly say "Yes" or "No" but only mumble and are so slow in decision-making. The cultures still differ radically. "We would love to have someone like Sen Nishiyama, who understands both cultures perfectly, come over and mediate, talk to us," says Morimoto. "But we are coming a lot closer anyway."

Morimoto still values meetings. When Sony San Diego

gave a fifteen-cent across-the-board raise last June, against the general economic trend, he brought workers together again, in groups of fifty or fewer, and told them why management was doing this. The cost of living had gone up, but they were especially interested in encouraging an increased concern for quality. "We hoped something fresh would develop."

Morimoto says: "You can't be out of touch. We spend less time in our offices than out on the floor"—where, as I saw, the workers all know him and seem genuinely affectionate when they say, "Hi, Mike." "And we are not hesitant about correcting mistakes if we have made them—which we do": not as a management ploy but because they want the plant to run well.

How do American workers compare with those in Japan?

"Our people work as well as their Japanese counterparts," says Morimoto.

Morimoto and other managers in San Diego remain strongly committed to the principle of avoiding layoffs, though there is no outright guarantee of lifetime employment. To accommodate fluctuations in demand, they have done two things: shifted workers temporarily to other positions when a line has to be shut down and built their own file of part-timers, so they can develop trained and dependable people rather than draw from general agencies.

There are some appealing upshots to what Kodera, Morimoto, and Dishno did in San Diego. In highly appreciative comments on the plant in a *Harvard Business Review* article, Richard Tanner Johnson and William G. Ouchi noted that "the company treated its employees as 'whole persons' rather than so many productive units. Not only is productivity at Sony high, but also absenteeism and turnover are low"—some 25 to 50 percent "below those at other electronics companies in that area."

Mark Espinosa, a line worker, says: "You are not just a body here. There is less pushing to make you work harder and more emphasis on quality." And another worker: "You get the feeling around here that they care about people!"

The expression on this San Diego line worker's face isn't a fraud: Work on the line is demanding and interesting, and the informal spirit that pervades the plant increases morale.

An aerial view of the impressive San Diego plant.

The color television assembly line in the Bridgend plant, Wales.

Today the San Diego plant produces about 28,000 Trinitrons a month; with Sonam pressing to secure 10 percent of the color television market by 1980, the plant will become increasingly important. But its significance transcends mere production figures: It has been—and remains—a fascinating experiment, and what Sony has learned there will be used in other offshore plants.

Already Sony is producing color television sets in Bridgend, Wales, and has purchased Wega Radio in Stuttgart, Germany, and revised production there; it is planning to build a plant in France; by 1977, it will have a tape plant in Dothan,

The Bridgend plant.

Alabama. A distributor in Cape Town is assembling, under contract with Sony (to buy parts and secure technical help) 60,000 Trinitrons a year; there are joint manufacturing or assembling agreements in Singapore, Thailand, Taiwan, Korea, Spain, Nigeria, and elsewhere.

"Eventually," says Morita, "we must become international at our headquarters. It is increasingly important to keep the whole world in view at all times."

So the experiment continues, increasingly international in scope.

CHAPTER ELEVEN

Morita Today

To play a role in the world other than that of traveling salesman, Japan needs people who can talk to foreigners, live with foreigners, relax in the presence of foreigners, argue with them, and arouse their enthusiasm.

—FRANK GIBNEY

L ITHE, SILVER-HAIRED, dressed in tight-fitting continental clothes, with bright wide eyes and inexhaustible energy, outspoken and surely speaking often enough—at Harvard, on Wall Street, in Manila, Chicago, Boston, Washington, in England, in all corners of Japan—Akio Morita, at fifty-five, is the most visible Japanese businessman in the world. He is not only admirably suited to such employment but loves it dearly.

He is known primarily as a salesman, and this, in the broadest sense of the word, is his most obvious role. He has the knowledge, the confidence, and the tenacity to persuade. He can sell the idea of joining Sony to new, talented men he needs, the inevitable sales of Betamax to groups of perhaps doubting dealers, and he has sold the tape recorder, transistor radio, microtelevision, Trinitron, and a host of other electronic firsts, and now video tape recording to the world. Vincent Hanna, the British journalist, found this constant salesmanship *de trop*. After a long day with Morita, he said: "If you believe him, you can come to tell yourself that life is meaningless without his gadgetry around you. Listen to him for long enough and the world is a small screen designed in Japan and made at Bridgend by Sony."

Sometimes Morita sounds brash, even audacious. "We don't believe in market research for a new product. We are the experts. We should know what technology can be turned into consumer products." Though in the long run he has usually managed to be proved right, some outside observers have considered this bold self-confidence the source of such Sony errors as the Chromatron; one said, "He stays when most people would have *run* from that disaster."

He has an unfailing flair for promotion. When he introduced the video camera in the late 1960s, a reporter from *Newsweek* came to interview him in the Sony offices at Fifth Avenue and Forty-seventh Street. While they talked, Morita looked out the window and noticed smoke coming out of the grate in front of the Sony showroom across the street. Within seconds, a fire engine had arrived. Morita excused himself briskly, grabbed the video camera, and ran out. The reporter and Ira Morais looked at each other in wild surmise, then saw Morita across the street with his camera; five minutes later he was back in the office. "Now," he said, "I'm going to show you how to have instant replay."

A few days later, when a reporter from the *New York Times* came for an interview, the same thing happened and

Morita is an inveterate demonstrator!

Morita again raced out. (Ironically, when he was demonstrating the Trinitron on a lower level in the Americana Hotel, a subway fire sent smoke into the display area, causing the *Times* reporter to comment, "Morita's playing with matches again.")

Hanna traveled with Morita to one of the yearly dealer conferences—twelve of which, each with two to four hundred participants, are held in January throughout Japan. It is a tradition of long standing and an important feature of Sony's communication of basic concepts. The journalist saw Morita's Abercrombie & Fitch overcoat, "Italian-shod" feet, and a brash ebullience that could affirm, even though there was heavy snow: "They'll come. I'm famous." He saw the meeting, for the dealers, as "two days away from the shop, a lot of free sake, and a free photograph with their leader thrown in."

I made the same trip, not to Sapporo but to Fukuoka, at the opposite end of Japan, and though the details were similar —including the trip in Morita's beloved Cessna twin-jet Citation, the first company jet in Japan—I saw something different. In the early 1950s, when he tried to sell the tape recorder through distributors, Morita realized that there was one relay station too many; these dealer meetings provided an invaluable link—to the new products and concepts that grew from top management, even to Morita himself. He *is* charismatic—and knows it.

I don't think Morita thought of these meetings in terms of "like" or "dislike," only as necessary. There is a oneness in the man between himself and his company. It was a thing to be done, which would take considerable time and much energy. But his words—spoken with verve and clarity—would provide the dealers with a convincing logic for selling (this year) the Betamax: A printed memo would not have done the same job. The bowing was traditional, not sycophantic. The breaking of the first sake barrel of the year seemed a happy custom. The hundreds of photographs with Morita, under special lights, would be pleasant mementos—and valuable in the shops. Morita was maintaining a connection with thousands of his salesmen, a job more and more difficult as Sony has grown larger. He was merely the best man to do the job.

Morita redeems the notion of leadership. Surely he is not the typical gray Japanese corporation president—as he says, with a light laugh, "old, deaf, and silent"—from whom little policy (or anything else) emanates; but neither is he the square-jawed American or German leader, inaccessible, even dictatorial, who falls into what Peter Drucker calls "the fallacy of the *Unternehmer*," the boss beside whom all others are merely technicians.

A leader. Not a boss.

The difference is illuminating.

Edward F. Rosiny, who has worked for and beside him in scores of negotiations, and has seen him function in Sony of

Morita with his American attorney, Edward F. Rosiny.

America, says: "The man has remarkable personal qualities. He never speaks down; he knows how to encourage the best in those who work for him; he can listen well, change his mind without feeling he is losing face, and finally, when necessary, be decisive." Rosiny says he has never seen Morita angry with a staff member, has never heard him make a disparaging remark to an employee. But what most impresses him, as a human and managerial strength, is Morita's loyalty. He can be tough in negotiations, capable of saying to an adversary (and meaning it), "We will give nothing," but he stands by friends strongly. "He gives and begets loyalty."

From the first months Rosiny represented Sony in American negotiations, Morita gave him total support. In one of his first—and an extremely tense—conferences, only a short time after he was retained, Rosiny presented Sony's position in unflinching terms, and held that position while his adversary tried first soft sell (praising Sony, inviting Rosiny and Morita to dinner that night), "then grew hard, then rough, and finally blew his top." The man turned to the translator and asked him, at some length, to tell Morita that he had hoped Morita would negotiate directly—that he did not want to deal with Rosiny. The translator took three pages of notes, then spoke to Morita in Japanese.

A moment later, in Japanese, Morita said: "I want you to know that I heard and understood every word you said. And I want you to know that everything Mr. Rosiny said I would have said." The man blanched. Morita continued, supporting each point Rosiny had made, and finally ended: "More than anything, I deeply resent your disparaging comments about Mr. Rosiny, and have just remembered that we have other commitments tonight and cannot have dinner with you."

And with that, he got up and walked out with Rosiny (who, some years later, with a more prudent negotiator from the same firm, made a brilliant settlement).

This is loyalty from a hard-hitting businessman. But there are other, purely human, examples. Sony is Morita's family and those in it are part of that family. He is loyal to affections and feelings. When "Doc" Kagawa, a Nisei Hawaiian who served as executive liaison for many years, fractured his skull in a car accident on Long Island, Morita called two and three times a day from Tokyo, kept in regular contact with Kagawa's family in Hawaii, as if Kagawa was one of his family. "This surprised no one," says Irving Sagor, "nobody expected otherwise of him."

Morita's loyalty is so much taken for granted at Sony that I learned only by chance of another striking instance. After his friend Shido Yamada died in 1957, Morita at once found Mrs. Yamada work and arranged for a young man to travel to her apartment on Knox Place in the Bronx every day to help her shop; when Sonam was formed, with a handful of people, he made sure she had a job. On anniversaries of Yamada's death, Morita has found time to visit his grave on Long Island, and to leave a traditional plant. To this day Mrs. Makie Yamada works for Sonam, and only last year, nearly twenty years after her husband's death, Morita convinced her to continue coming in at least a few days a week—not wanting her to be alone or to lose her connection with the firm. He invites her to executive cocktail parties, and sends her a white corsage. I met Mrs. Yamada at such a party: She is a diminutive woman (under five feet, I think), charming and over sixty, and much loved by other members of the firm—including one much younger American executive, well over six feet, who says with warm affection, "If I didn't have a good wife already, I'd marry Mrs. Yamada!" Another adds: "Morita has made a life for her here—without a touch of charity involved. Would Sarnoff have done that?"

"Though you always know he is running the show," one vice-president told me, "he never steps on your toes. He will say, 'Here's my concept,' and paint a broad brush picture. Then: 'That's my philosophy.' He doesn't say you should do a *specific* thing but gives you the flexibility to get the job done yourself."

He *sees* and knows his adjutants as independent people,

This American conference includes Rosiny, Morita, Iwama, and Inagaki.

has (I'm told, and saw) an astounding capacity to keep in touch with middle and lower-level employees, and is willing to put his trust in them. He is rarely disappointed. At production plants in Japan and America, in the offices of Japanese and American middle managers, I heard stories of such trust—and of men working harder than they had ever worked before.

"At first you listen to him," says Ray Steiner, "and think you can second-guess him. But then you don't try to second-guess him anymore because what he said is what happened. He seems to be making snap judgments—until you realize that he anticipated your question months ago. Other presidents give you a picture based on the market that's out there, and say, 'Do this and this and this'; Morita gives you a broad picture of what the market will be two, three, or ten years from today. And he is right."

Is he *always* right?

"Usually," says Steiner, "and when he's not, he will listen

to you and change his mind beforehand, or admit that he said something else six months ago but has changed his thinking."

Not for him a foolish consistency. He is large; he really does contain multitudes. And curiously he *does* have that Emersonian, Whitmanesque fluidity: It is, for me, a rare and happy quality in a captain of industry.

Many American executives are sadly skeptical of such fluidity and trust—or merely incapable of it; they say it smacks of soft-mindedness. Executives fear they will lose their authority; they are afraid to delegate because they worry that their power base will be eroded; they fear to change their minds because this will make them lose face; they fear an open-door policy because impersonality builds and retains power.

Fear. There is a lot of fear in high places.

Morita knows that to attract and hold the kind of executives he wants he must do more than "buy" them; he knows, to use Drucker's criteria, that such people are "not productive under the spur of fear," that only "self-motivation and self-direction" can make them productive.

More Drucker is applicable here: "Leadership is the lifting of a man's vision to higher sights, the raising of a man's performance to a higher standard, the building of a man's personality beyond its normal limitations." Remember Suzuki in New York in 1960, Ohga in Tokyo, Morimoto in San Diego? I met others with similar stories. Such a philosophy—which cannot be a "trick" of management—works.

There are those, says Drucker, who see only weakness and thus destroy people, spirit, and performance; but a true manager "develops people, including himself." Amen.

Personally, Morita is remarkably protean; he is neither (as he has been called) a Westernized Japanese nor Japanese on the outside, Western inside. He is very much Japanese—from his love of a traditional breakfast in Fukuoka to his respect for deeper Japanese customs and traditions; but he is, today, an internationalist, and being such, he is a chameleon.

Morita and his wife relax near the window of his office at 9 West Fifty-seventh Street in New York City.

The Moritas with Arthur Stanton of Volkswagen; Stanton introduced Morita to William Bernbach, who launched the successful "tummy TV" ads for Sony. *Photo by Paul Schumach*

Hosting a cocktail party in his New York offices at 9 West Fifty-seventh Street, you can see him standing with his wife at the entrance greeting the newly arrived. He is wearing a light tan continental suit with widely flared trouser bottoms. As always, his silver hair is parted in the middle. Traditional Japanese do not touch each other or show deep affection in public; a Japanese enters and Morita's smile vanishes. He faces the man formally and bows deeply at the waist, then deeper, then up slightly—the expression serious, the stance reverent, both men silent—then deep again, to his knees, and deeper still. It is a customary bow, a deeply ingrained gesture that he performs instinctively. Does he realize how curious it looks to a Westerner, how stiff and unaccommodating it appears?

A moment later he is up and smiling widely to an American friend, his hand out, shaking the other's hand, then grasping the friend's arm or shoulder with his free hand—chatting, laughing, still pumping the hand. The change has been immediate. There has been no clanking of shifted gears. (One American manager conjectured that when he spoke in London, his maverick American-English probably took on an English accent.)

Is there a trace of hypocrisy on his face? Some hint of corporate fakery?

Surely there must be.

I look closely. Like Fra Lippo Lippi, hiding in one of his own paintings, I stand to the side where I can scarcely be seen—and I stare, unabashedly.

The chameleon's nature is to be protean, changeable with terrain, environment. So is the politician's.

Morita today is at home in almost every corner of the world, with scores of different tasks and commitments and people. Since 1953 he has crossed the Pacific more than 125 times—he has lost count. He loves to walk through the streets of foreign cities, peering into shops. He is a whirligig of motion. He opens the Bridgend plant with the Prince of Wales, zips up to the Harvard Business School to deliver an extemporaneous talk, has an early morning breakfast conference in Tokyo with a reporter for a major newsweekly, dines with President and Mrs. Marcos in Manila, flies to Fukuoka to speak with several hundred dealers, meets with the Board of IBM/World Trade (of which he is a director, and a director too of Americas/Far East Corporation, and an adviser to All-Nippon Airways), phones all over the world, takes the Robert Ingersolls to his country home for the weekend, dines at Maxim's in the Sony building with his eighty-two-year-old mother and ten other members of the Morita clan (including Iwama, who is married to his sister), golfs in Honolulu (where he has an apartment), designs his own golf clubs (hoping to reduce his 16 handicap, and writes an article on the subject called "More Pleasurable 'My Own Golf' with Self-Designed, Handmade Clubs of Uniform Length, Hammer-shaped for a Sure Hit"), holds a Sunday afternoon executive meeting in his home study (fitted with a conference table and chairs), attends a concert or musical, likes it, arranges to have *Fiddler on the Roof* brought to Japan, studies his fiercely competitive industry, meets with four hundred Sony managers once a month, inspects the San Diego plant and speaks with the line workers, serves on a government commission to study strikes by government employees, sleeps a few hours (I suppose), and starts again.

In his spare time he collects American antiques, including old nickelodeons and player pianos. In more spare time, last year, he sat down with Konosuke Matsushita, his octogenarian friend and the founder of the massive Matsushita Electric, and they talked for seven hours about politics, the effect of the American Occupation, the decline of youth, the state of the economy; the talk is taped and then published as *Yuron* (A Concerned Dialogue), and promptly sells 250,000 copies. In the sixties he also wrote *Gakureki Muyo-ron* (Never Mind School Records) and *Shin Jitsuryoku Shugi* (A New Merit System)—both of which were sensations in Japan.

TIME

How to Cope With

JAPAN'S BUSINESS INVASION

Sony's Akio Morita

One can only be startled, even perplexed at the source of so much energy, which at least one manager said exhausted him to watch. At a dinner meeting I had with Morita one evening in Tokyo, he had to skip off at nine for a business conference, and then was scheduled to leave at six the next morning for a dealer's meeting in snowbound Sapporo. When, after our ample meal, he ordered ice cream for dessert, he explained that he needed to keep up his energy.

I was pleased to know this, somehow.

Morita is a man of many opinions:

On the will to work: "The inherent spiritual support of men is lacking more than ever in recent times. The will to work is being frustrated, and people speak as though it is almost meaningless to work."

On discipline: "A nation whose people are disciplined will steadily grow, and a nation that lacks discipline will decline."

On the American Occupation: "By abolishing the very valuable moral education, we have developed a younger generation devoid of any ethical or moral value system."

On Japan: "A small country, poor in resources, with a population of over 100 million, has only one way to go if she is not to be a permanent burden on other nations for economic aid. That way is for the people to use their brains, utilize technology, and work hard."

On teamwork: "Business is not an individual game, it is teamwork. Nothing can be accomplished without harmonious collaboration."

On management's chief goal: "Sony must be a place where people in the prime of their lives can work to the fullest."

On the history of innovations: "Once people asked me, 'Why would anyone want to record voices?' Now everyone has a tape recorder. Even an American president had to resign because of a tape recorder."

On *mottainai* (the concept that everything in the world must be taken care of with precious attention): "Everything must be carefully used, never wasted, nor used more than neces-

A quiet moment in Morita's large New York office.

sary . . . all things, no matter how small, are provided as a sacred trust and are sacred loans to men for use in their lives."

On America's *lack* of *mottainai:* "If Americans applied a word like *'mottainai,'* their whole economic structure would collapse."

On all that has come before: "What I have said so far reflects my way of thinking only up to the present moment. I cannot tell how it may change in the future."

When not on one of his frequent and far-flung trips, Morita lives with his wife and teen-age daughter, Naoko, in a twenty-six-room mansion in Shibuya, a wealthy suburb of Tokyo; his two sons—neither of whom has plans to enter Sony —are now in American colleges, studying agriculture and business. His home, on a half-acre corner landscaped exquisitely with rocks, a profusion of flowers, bonsai trees, rhododendron bushes, and the traditional falling water, reflects the man. It is an unforgettable place, designed half by him, half by Mrs. Morita.

One journalist called the home "a cross between the Pan-Am Terminal at Kennedy Airport and Tiffany's showroom." Certainly it is as eclectic as the Moritas—and was built so that "Westerners would feel they had really been to Japan and Japanese could experience some place Western." Each room has its own character—Western, Eastern, or what at times seemed to me both at once.

The house sports a luxurious indoor swimming pool (at which Leonard Bernstein likes to relax when he visits) and a traditional Japanese bath; there is a rooftop observation post, reached from an outside circular stairway, from which you can see Mount Fuji; a multitude of hi-fi and stereo units are connected to some *200* loudspeakers; there is a magnificent 1910 player piano on which you can hear (and see the finger depressions of) George Gershwin playing "Rhapsody in Blue" or Rachmaninoff one of his own preludes. Upon insertion of the mandatory nickel, the genuine old nickelodeon grinds up and plays "Columbia, the Gem of the Ocean." The dining room—done in black and white so that guests dressed in any colors will not clash—is built for large dinners, of which there are many: Has not Mrs. Morita written *My Thoughts on Home Entertaining?* The traditional eight-tatami mat room has held Japanese royalty.

It is a busy house.

It is a house that obviously gives the Moritas much pleasure—with its curious mixture of the elegant and the informal, the lavish and the comfortable, East and West; it is a place that very much begs to be talked about.

The Moritas' living room in Tokyo. To the right of the fireplace, which Morita designed, is a baby grand player piano imported from New York. In the background is a library for music albums, 1,000 player-piano rolls, and an elaborate hi-fi system. The ceiling is fishnet.

As I sit in my own rather small New York City apartment, crowded mostly with books and my wife's paintings, trying to find a corner of the six rooms where one of my four children is not parked or barking, I try to gain a clear, objective view of Morita today.

The view has much motion. Video cameras. Ohga. Charlie Farr. Mrs. Yamada. The Harvard Business School. Fukuoka. The Cessna Citation. They are all there. But within the kaleidoscope, somehow, I keep seeing Morita leaving the dinner table in the Sony building and walking to the thermostat, which is broken. He putters with it for a moment, then, with a bold laugh, proclaims: "I can fix anything."

CHAPTER TWELVE

The Age of Betamax

There is only one valid definition of business purpose: to create a customer.

—PETER F. DRUCKER

When we have a fine new product, we must have the courage to introduce it to the market.

—AKIO MORITA

VIDEO TAPE recording for consumer use has a rotten record. CBS reportedly lost $30 million on its Electronic Video Recording (EVR), an $800 device that permitted viewers to play movie cartridges on their television sets. Ampex tried and was not able to launch a home-video unit. Cartridge Television's Cartrivision, one of the largest financial debacles of the past decade, played movies and, by a skip-field method, could record television programs; it lost $60 million.

The Betamax, Sony's latest major product, is also a video-

202

recording device for home use—and the company has committed itself so completely to its development, production, and sale that many staff members in Tokyo wear VTR cuff links and badges.

This is another bold, even daring gesture.

No sooner was it announced than *The Gallagher Report,* "a confidential letter to marketing, sales, advertising, and media executives," headlined a news item: "SONY MAKES MARKETING MISTAKE," and homed in on Morita's little habit of not doing prior market research. The report found Sony's equation of the video with the audio-tape market fallacious and called the whole venture a "long-shot gamble."

It is a bold gesture, indeed—but one that had its origins nearly twenty-five years ago.

As early as 1952, before they had developed the transistorized radio, Sony engineers began to monitor and translate articles related to the video field. The company had already committed itself to the production of its own magnetic tape for audio tape recorders, and this would in time provide it with an important branch of the technology needed for video recording.

Video was in the air. Everyone could sense its importance. But the technology was highly complicated and its precise uses and marketing possibilities were ambiguous.

In the 1950s, Ampex, the foremost firm in video recording, produced a four-head machine that sold for over $100,000; its principal sales were to broadcasting stations, where it promptly began to replace film. Soon afterward, discussions began between top management at Ampex and Sony, in which it was anticipated that Sony would develop a much less expensive machine. The relationship between the two companies was so friendly that, on July 10, 1960, without benefit of counsel, Morita, Ibuka, and a vice-president of Ampex signed a one-page memorandum indicating a free royalty exchange of their firm's respective patents, including Ampex's seminal Ginsburg patent (a system that converts a video signal to FM signals, then records it on tape).

Within months, a team of engineers headed by Kihara produced Sony's first important VTR. Though this initial two-head, open-reel model was heavy and had not nearly the fidelity of Ampex's four-head machine, it represented the first step in a series of forthcoming achievements for Sony in the video field. Also, its price was almost one-tenth that of Ampex's $100,000 VTR, and it had a tremendous effect on the market. Many National Football League teams bought the machine to play back practice sessions; Pan-American Airlines and American Airlines used sets to show takeoffs and landings to

The AV-3650, an early reel-to-reel video tape recorder.

passengers; a Sony subsidiary called Video-Flight was established to provide in-flight movies.

But major shifts in top management at Ampex had meanwhile led to a serious dispute concerning the meaning and intent of the July 10 memorandum. New agreements were drawn up, including—at first—a provision that Sony must pay an 8 percent royalty for the use of the Ginsburg patent, but no mutually satisfactory solution could be found. The situation was critical. Without the use of the Ginsburg patent, Sony might not be able to remain in the video field.

While discussions continued, year after year, Sony introduced a second VTR in 1964, designated the EV Series, which sold for approximately $3,000, then the TCV 2020 and 2110 in 1965 at $1,200, and in 1966 the first low-priced compact VTR, the CV-2000. The price of the CV was $800, less than one hundredth of the cost of Ampex's first machine; it used ½-inch magnetic tape (reel-to-reel), and it could record in black and white for 60 minutes. The price, and the fact that the machine was portable, represented an awesome breakthrough.

After six years, Sony and Ampex made an amiable settlement of their dispute; today they are on exceptionally good terms. Sony was now free to concentrate its fullest resources on the development of video tape recording. From the beginning, Ibuka says, Sony's target was a unit that would eventually find its principal use in the home: They were coming closer to that goal.

The U-Matic video cassette, Sony's next major product in this field, was introduced in 1969 and soon became successful —and standard—in America. Substantial numbers were sold, at $1,000 each, for use in the educational, business, and medical fields. The Ford Motor Co. purchased 5,000 units for corporate communications and merchandising.

The U-Matic became especially attractive, instead of 16mm film, for news gathering: It was portable, it eliminated high film-development costs, it could easily be edited (especially with Sony's new electronic editing machine), and it could bring

The UV-340 video tape recorder.

The U-Matic video cassette.

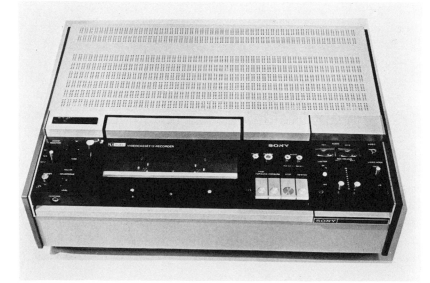

news stories to the viewer in much less time and at a savings of 70 to 80 percent to the station. So far, Sony has sold more than 200,000 U-Matics. They have not only been a profitable venture in themselves but have established Sony's reliability in the video tape recording field.

But all this was only prelude to the development of the Betamax for home use. It represents not only the culmination of twenty years of intense work in the video field but the accumulated technological skill and integration of virtually every Sony specialty—tapes, radio, circuitry, semiconductors, recording heads, television receivers, digital systems, video recording.

The differences between the units are significant. Whereas the U-Matic used ¾-inch tape, the Betamax tape is only ½ inch and fits into a less expensive cassette the size of a paperback book; this is made possible by using extrathin tape (only 20 microns thick), employing a very narrow head (the effective width of the recording track is about 60 microns), and reducing the tape speed to only 1.57 inches per second compared to the 3.75 inches per second for the U-Matic. The Betamax is simpler to operate. It is much more compact. Its tape consumption is less and its tape cost $15.95 against the U-Matic's $30.

Again the question: Will it sell?

Clearly the same kind of problems exist with the Betamax that Morita faced twenty-five years ago with the tape recorder: Would people find value in it? Would they find *enough* value to buy it?

Since the Japanese are avid televiewers with generally high-quality programs to view—including many special historical and educational series—and since more than 90 percent of Japanese households own a color television, Morita decided to introduce Betamax in Japan first. (Though this was traditionally the case with its earlier products, where flaws and operating problems could be removed before export was started, today the choice of whether to market in Japan first or market simultaneously is based purely on marketing considerations, not quality.) He also decided to introduce both a console

The Betamax video cassette console model for the American market.

The Betamax video cassette deck (SL-7300) with self-contained TV tuner—
and a Trinitron color TV set and Betamax video cassettes.

Trinitron-and-Betamax unit and a separate Betamax deck in Japan at the same time. The first products reached the Japanese market in May 1975 and consumer response was immediately strong. Samplings showed that most buyers fell into the twenty-five to thirty-five age group, with forty-five to fifty-five second; a large number of railway workers and airline pilots, who had odd working hours and would naturally miss prime-time shows, bought either the console or the separate deck.

For a number of reasons it was decided to market the combined unit first in America, in November 1975, and then follow with the separate deck in February 1976. It was felt that the Trinitron would provide the best results, but also the console would establish the higher price, which would then make the less expensive deck (which can be attached to any set for 50¢ worth of parts) more attractive.

Timing and target were deliberate. They had not felt, several years earlier, that the market was quite ready for home VTR; and they felt, as Morita told a Boston security analysts' meeting in February 1975, that everyone else had failed because they had only experimented, without adequate conviction or experience. Sony waited and improved its product and planned.

Frank Stanton, former president of CBS, accounted for part of their failure with EVR by suggesting: "We couldn't think of any kind of programs to ask people to buy that they couldn't get free on regular television." CBS, say some Sony executives, put the cart before the horse: They attempted to establish a software market before there were enough playback units in homes. They could not do it.

Sony also wanted to market a perfected product, and to have trained servicemen available for possible repair. Cartrivision, they felt, not only depended upon available software but also produced a shoddy product; and Sony's tape is half the cost of theirs. Also, Cartrivision was "oversold"; though some of the old Doyle Dane Bernbach wit was present in ads like "BETAMAX . . . the play it again Sony," the company is positioning itself cautiously in this new market, appealing to select, even affluent, televiewers—the ads are generally more informative, more sober. "We are still trying to see exactly what the need is," says Mort Fink, Sonam's advertising director, "and then we will develop our promotion to meet that need."

Joseph S. Wright, chairman of Zenith, has said: "The low-cost disk is where the real future is." But Sony has bypassed the disk in favor of tape; they feel that the $15.95 cost of an hour's cassette is not going to be prohibitive and that the operating advantages are substantial. "RCA, Philips, and Teledeck are all trying to get licensees for their disks," notes Iwama. "If they really wanted to establish their system, they should be willing to put in the required investment and take the necessary risk themselves." He adds: "We feel we must do it ourselves; it is a new system and a new market and we are not relying on other companies to do the job for us. Afterward, we may license; not now."

Sony's plan is, then, to market a highly developed product that is simple to use, and to educate the market first in its most logical use: as a time-shift machine for recording one's own programs on convenient cassettes. Later, the Time-Life and other libraries of software will come into their own, but first there must be sets available to play them on.

But how does Morita intend to get the Betamax units into the hands of enough viewers to begin with?

He begins, as always, with three ingredients: enthusiasm, total commitment to his product, and a shrewd knowledge of its possible uses. "You listen to Morita talk about the Betamax," says one Sonam executive, "and you come away with the feeling that you simply cannot live without it." Morita persuades from the inside out: his own managers, his dealers—and then the world.

"Betamax will revolutionize television," he says bluntly. "It will change the concept of prime time so that *any* time can be prime time. Before the development of video recording, television was too fleeting. While it has been outstanding for conveying information, providing entertainment, and improving our culture, the sad fact exists that once a program is off the air it is gone forever for the TV viewer. Newspapers, magazines, and books can be read and kept for future reference. But this had not been so with TV programs seen in the home."

Betamax will free us from the "time tyranny"; we will be able to watch when *we* want to watch, or can watch. Instead of adjusting our daily schedule to fit the convenience of the programmers, we can view it at *our* convenience. If your phone rings, you can stop the playback and make the program wait for you.

You can build your own library of programs.

Those without disciplined split vision can record one program while watching another.

To the question many Americans would ask, "Why should we *want* to record such dreadful programs?" he answers: "When tape is in front of a person he will become more careful of what he says. Telecasting companies will produce better programs when they know they are being recorded. And advertisers will *demand* better programs so their ad will be seen again and again on playback." (That is, if viewers do not use the "pause" button on their Betamax, which can eliminate commercials when a program is being recorded.)

The unit is as easy to operate as a tape recorder.

It can play prerecorded tapes, which, in the future, will become an important feature of the market. Time-Life already has a substantial library of such historic moments as the first moon walk, World Series finals, major concerts, Super Bowl games.

At a press conference Morita especially pointed to the new flurry of series on American television. A "hooked" viewer could record an episode he might otherwise miss.

Sometime in the future, Sony or another company will produce a viable color camera for home use, which will record home movies on tape cassettes that can then be shown on the television screen.

Sonam began to sell the Betamax in only thirteen cities at

first—New York, Washington, Philadelphia, Atlanta, Miami, Dallas, Chicago, Cleveland, Detroit, San Diego, Los Angeles, San Francisco, and Seattle. Steiner says that he would not permit the console to be sold to a dealer who did not take a training course in its use, and that proper servicing facilities had to be established *before* the product reached the market. (So far, reliability has been so high that there are fewer service problems than for a tape recorder.)

At $1,300 for the deck and $2,295 for the console, the Betamax has had only modest success in America so far. Morita remains confident. The home-video market has developed more slowly than he or any of the other companies had believed it would, but he *knows* that in time it will. "American businessmen try to cash in immediately," he says. "They have to make money. But we know that VTR will be important in the future and we are willing to invest now for that time." Yoshii adds: "No one yet believes it will work within five years, but someone has to be the guinea pig." Sony has been there before.

In Japan 25,000 were sold in the first six months; though they are now producing 10,000 a month, Sony has been backordered since June 1975. In 1976 they expect to produce 100,000 units; there are no immediate plans to produce the Betamax in the United States, though should the demand develop quickly, the new Dothan plant will be able to produce the necessary tapes.

Some people claim that the price of the Betamax in the United States will restrict its growth. But Robert Czepiel has made up a chart listing the average disposable income per capita in America when the black-and-white television was introduced in the early 1950s, when color came in, and today. With inflation, the $1,300 for the Betamax deck is only a scant few percentage points higher than the 29 percent a $400 black-and-white or the 25 percent a $600 color television once represented. A revealing figure.

Czepiel has also charted two conservative growth curves for Sony, based on either the success or failure of the Betamax.

The situation this time is different. Sony is no longer as dependent upon the success of this product as it was, say, on the success of the transistor radio or the Trinitron. Its product base is broader today, its annual report infinitely better balanced. Betamax *could* lead to a 15 to 20 percent annual growth in sales, Czepiel predicts, but if it does not succeed, the curve will merely be less dramatic, 10 to 15 percent.

The entrance of other companies into the home-video market, which Sony is not depending upon, can only increase the possibility of the concept's succeeding. RCA is preparing to market its Selectavision this year and MCA/Philips and Zenith are developing an "optical system." Prominent Japanese firms, such as Matsushita, will enter the home-video field as well.

Sony is prepared for a sudden explosion of interest. If Betamax really catches on, its Kohda plant near Nagoya can—on short notice—tool up to produce 30,000 units a month if necessary. A Sony subsidiary has been formed to acquire and rent software for the Betamax, and 3M has announced its intention to supply magnetic tape in the Betamax format. (Tape consumption is averaging about twelve cassettes per Betamax today.) With 60 million television sets currently in American homes, the stakes are large. If the home VTR idea is established, sales could be enormous.

Sony has also been pioneering the possibility of bringing the Betamax into underdeveloped countries, where it has unique uses. Masaaki Morita, one of Morita's younger brothers, has been especially interested in promoting such ventures.

Masaaki Morita joined the firm in 1951, after studying electrochemistry in college. He, like his brother, was expected to enter his father's sake-brewing firm in Nagoya but "had always been interested in innovations—and my father's firm had been making the same thing for three centuries." He became an expert in magnetic tape and spent sixteen years at the Sendei tape plant until Ibuka told him one day: "Find a staff

and find yourself a place to work. We would like you to discover new marketing areas where Sony can become active other
than the established mass markets."

With shrewd initiative, Masaaki Morita established contact with the Shah of Iran's twin sister, and with Ibuka's encouragement the princess signed a contract with Sony by which
fourteen Iranian candidate teachers would be trained in electronics at the Atsugi plant and then Sony would help to create
a training center in Iran that could train 1,000 technicians a
year.

Masaaki Morita is also centrally involved with a project
concerning President and Mrs. Marcos and the Philippines
government for the development of a major video network
throughout the islands. Though it is almost a fad among developing nations to use communications satellites to telecast
programs and information down into the back country, the
Philippines has apparently found the Betamax a more efficient,
economical, and effective way of reaching the hinterlands. In
1975 Sony signed an agreement with Mrs. Marcos, and is already shipping hardware into twenty villages that will be used
for a pilot trial; if the system works, every hamlet and village
on the 7,100 islands will soon have a Betamax unit.

If the satellite method had been chosen, everyone would
have had to watch when the program was telecast; also, with
cassettes, each district will be able to supplement major programs with local news—and a two-track tape will allow different
languages to be used; the Betamax project will also require
only a small generator where electricity is scarce or unavailable.

The government is already considering family-planning
programs for housewives, educational programs for children,
and policy statements and speeches for husbands. Sony will
help teach the government how to make their own software.

Is all this prelude to 1984? To the conditioning of developing peoples through the use of sophisticated modern
technology? Is it the final rape of indigenous cultures that
Melville foresaw in his earliest novels, *Typee* and *Omoo?*

Difficult questions.
But questions that must be asked.

What, finally, are the prospects for the Betamax?
Morita thinks, of course, that eventually the same percentage of people will want video as now own audio tape
recorders. He began precisely at zero with the tape recorder.
He is convinced we are now entering the Age of Betamax.

Czepiel, who is known as the guru on Sony among the
stock analysts, has studied the VTR situation with great care.
He also knows Morita, and has watched his enthusiasm for
home-video recording wax eloquent these past years. "If Betamax does not go," says Czepiel, "it will mean there is simply
no home-video market."

The phenomenon should be exciting to follow.

EPILOGUE

The Next Thirty Years

The myth of Sony has not collapsed; it never was a myth. But the myth of continuing high growth rates around the world is over.

—AKIO MORITA

Sony cannot afford to live off its name like an octopus eating its own tentacles.

—NORIO OHGA

I T IS tempting to look back to the good old days," Morita told a roomful of managers recently, "but when you do this, that's the end of the company."

Sony has much to look back on with pride: Its scores of firsts in a highly competitive field; its extraordinary growth from those first days in the burned-out Shirokiya department store; wise management that has led so many of its employees to work to the fullest of their capacity; an international reputa-

216

tion for quality. Though it has advanced dramatically from rice cookers to riches, the company has maintained a remarkable loyalty to the spirit with which it was founded thirty years ago.

"A company must not have a limit to its life," Morita said. "My management policy, the basic spirit of Sony, must continue without limit." This is a hard motto to live up to for an electronics firm that has undergone such radical growth.

Clearly there are changes—in Sony and in the world around it.

Nationally, Japan is still struggling desperately, after three hard years, to regain the economic equilibrium it lost during the energy crisis. The hopes for an upturn after the summer of 1975 were not realized; the government, which with severity held inflation down to 10 percent, was plagued by an illegal and crippling strike over the right to strike by government employees. Even that basic institution, lifetime employment, was threatened: Four hundred employees of one firm "voluntarily retired" after its leaders announced its financial predicament; some companies, for the first time, were even forced to lay off employees—Yashica dismissed 900 of its 2,200 workers. And unemployment reached its worst level in sixteen years—and is still worsening. The Japanese, said Andrew Malcolm in the *New York Times,* "are experiencing the longest and deepest recession since World War II." More than 30 percent of the nation's leading corporations went into the red, and by December 1975 there was a record number of bankruptcies.

The pinch, of course, is not restricted to Japan. In fact, with the new internationalism of Japan-based multinationals, when Thorn Electrical, an RCA-affiliated company in Lancashire, England, ran into financial difficulties in 1976, union representatives of its 1,400 employees sent an urgent telegram to Tadao Kato, ambassador to the United Kingdom, asking if a Japanese company would *please* like to take control. (Morita told me: "It's too expensive.")

Sony's position at this critical moment, in the year of

its thirtieth anniversary, is intriguing. They have for many years stressed that they are constantly building for the future. That future, and its complex challenges, is now here.

Surely the Sony name, which Morita and Ibuka were at such pains to establish, is unimpeachable. It has successfully weathered the general attacks on Japanese firms by foreign countries and its devotion to quality remains intact.

Though in early 1975 it was required—for the first time—to order an extra five-day "paid holiday" for 8,000 of its employees (at about 95 percent of their basic salaries), and to freeze starting wages, it was thus able this year to reduce its inventory by $82 million, purchase all the shares of Wega Radio in Stuttgart, establish several major new subsidiaries (Sony Arabia and Sony of Canada), break ground for a new tape plant in Dothan, Alabama, and introduce a major new product, the Betamax. It also brought a far more balanced distribution to its foreign sales figures (26 percent in America now, 14 percent in Europe, and 15 percent elsewhere).

In January 1976 it also changed its top management. Morita, at fifty-five, became chairman of the board and chief executive officer; Ibuka, at sixty-eight, became honorary chairman; and Iwama was elected president and chief operating officer. Ohga, now in his mid-forties, became deputy president while retaining his presidency of CBS-Sony and assuming wide responsibilities for international sales. Though several magazines in Japan tried to suggest a severe political upheaval in Sony, the changes were both predictable and logical. Ibuka, released from his day-to-day executive duties, will be free to oversee his deepest love: research and product development. Morita, who will continue to develop the concept and practice of internationalism, will perhaps travel more and become even more "visible" in international affairs; so doing, the immediate care of daily operations will fall to Iwama, still a vigorous young man in his mid-fifties, who has been with Sony since its earliest days and has long held positions of major responsibility. Ohga, who has proved so valuable in corporate finance,

Ibuka and Morita today.

negotiations, and product development and design, now has the broad executive skills needed to assume whatever top management duties he is called upon to perform.

A longtime American observer of Sony and the electronics industry asked me: "Is there anyone who could replace Morita?" Though it is much too early to worry about such an eventuality, my impression is that management at Sony is strong and deep; even many of the middle managers, in their late thirties and early forties, show executive promise—and have been broadly trained and wisely cross-trained. And the basic principles of the company are deeply ingrained now. But Morita, like all

The Osaka Sony tower, opened April 15, 1976.

unique individuals, is irreplaceable: His particular flair, his unflagging energy, his charisma, his unending flow of "concepts" —these are his alone.

Sony's challenges—in marketing, management, technology, finance, and morale—are now momentous.

Clearly, the company's marketing will be increasingly international in scope. Sony will continue to design products specifically for individual markets, and it will strive to become more and more intimate with each country's needs. It is vigorously seeking larger penetration of the lush American market, and will try to increase its current 7½ percent share of the color TV sales to 10 percent by 1980; it has already begun to expand in the audio field and in 1976 will launch a major campaign by its business machines division. Iwama stresses the special interest Sony has in the less developed markets. Color penetration in Europe, for instance, is still only 30 percent, and sales have only scratched the potential of South America, Australia, South Africa, and similar countries. China, Iwama feels, with its hundreds of millions of people, may someday prove a strong market—but not in the forseeable future.

Morita wants management to become increasingly international—with local nationals heading as many subsidiaries as possible and more and more internationally trained managers on the headquarters staff. This concept of management high-

An interior display at the Osaka Sony tower.

lights the necessity to communicate rapidly and accurately all needed information on international finance, stock markets, tax laws, sales, and servicing. To monitor the way Sony executives are managing the company, Morita recently established an executive advisory board, chaired by Ibuka and composed of outside experts. This represents, for Japan, another Sony first.

One international problem that especially concerns Morita is the "invisible nontariff barriers"—different standards for such factors as exhaust fumes, cycles of electricity, X-ray radioactivity, industrial safety, and the like. These, along with high import taxes, have made offshore production by knowledgeable nationals a must. Though he is pressing for global standardization of the "invisible barriers," he is aware that this ideal lies well in the future.

Though Sony's technology has always been exceptionally strong, the electronics industry remains severely competitive. "The harder the times become," says Morita, "the more vital becomes the factor of technology. Technology is the greatest tool to keep us viable." A major, increasingly difficult challenge will be to introduce bold new products like the Betamax, and maintain the courage to market them vigorously.

Financially, Sony must improve its earnings to attract new investors, 42 percent of whom are foreigners today. Reducing its inventory, cutting its short-term debt ratio, and establishing local credit ratings such as its recent AA from Standard & Poor will all help. Yoshii and Morita have also been in the forefront of those who want the Japanese government to change the required annual report to one that will be more comprehensible to foreign investors.

Perhaps the greatest challenge is to the spirit of the place, to its morale. Though with 20,000 employees it is still only one-fourth the size of a company like Matsushita (with more than 80,000 employees), the links Kobayashi spoke of are surely threatened. Morita giving a New Year's speech on video cassette is *not* Morita in person—but you cannot slice a man up 20,000 ways. The sophisticated management and technology could

Sony celebrates its thirtieth anniversary in May 1976, at San Diego, with a birthday cake in the form of its first magnetic tape recorder, Model G. *From left to right:* Ohga, Morita, Ray Steiner, and Harvey Schein.

cause narrow specialization; the need for cautious management —to protect the many investors who own shares in Sony— threatens the company's longtime love of risk. "Management must continue to work out new ways to preserve the boldness and imagination that have always characterized Sony," says Ohga. "While making sound and safe decisions, based on scientific data, our greatest challenge will be not to lose the fine edge that *challenge* itself provides."

In the late 1960s Richard Halloran said of Japan that "the financial underpinnings of the economy are shaky and held together with baling wire." He was proved right. The boom years are over; never again will the GNP increase as it did for more than two decades; with price controls and escalating costs of raw material, energy, and labor, gross sales will never again be so readily reflected in gross profit. "The fragile superpower" that Frank Gibney envisions has trembled to its core.

But though sorely challenged, Sony has now survived the worst and continued to grow. Its success formula has proved to contain both depth and balance.

In his New Year's talk to one group of managers, Morita told them they could not "mark time waiting for good times." They had to manage within what would hereafter be a more sober norm. But now that the high growth rates are over, there are new challenges, new opportunities.

"We do not expect an outside force to help us. We must be self-reliant. My great premise is always the spirit of free competition."

He and his company remain vigorous entrepreneurs—in an old, and I think good, sense.

"Everything still points to a new road, internationalism," he says. "We must now start to write the new story of Sony."

A Brief Selected Bibliography

The following books have especially helped me to understand Japan and Japanese business better

Barnet, Richard J., and Ronald E. Muller. *Global Reach.* New York: Simon and Schuster, 1974. A massive study of "the power of the multinational corporations."

Benedict, Ruth. *The Chrysanthemum and the Sword.* Boston: Houghton Mifflin, 1946. A fine study of Japanese character.

Busch, Noel F. *The Horizon Concise History of Japan.* New York: American Heritage, 1972. A helpful overview.

Doi, Takeo. *The Anatomy of Dependence.* Tokyo: Kodansha International, 1973. A penetrating look at *amae,* and how it functions in Japanese life, by a brilliant psychiatrist.

225

Drucker, Peter F. *Management*. New York: Harper & Row, 1974. A brilliant study by a master management consultant with frequent references to Sony.

Forbis, William H. *Japan Today*. New York: Harper & Row, 1975. Perhaps the most sensible, broad-based, and thorough look at Japan today.

Gibney, Frank. *Japan: The Fragile Superpower*. Tokyo: Charles E. Tuttle, 1975. Narrower in focus—and more sharply focused—than the Forbis, but more authoritative, challenging, and aware.

Halloran, Richard. *Japan: Images and Realities*. New York: Alfred A. Knopf, 1969. A superb book that demonstrates how, beneath its veneer of westernization, "the essence of Japanese life flows from ideas, ethics, customs, and institutions that are anchored deep in Japanese culture and history."

Kahn, Herman. *The Emerging Japanese Superstate*. Englewood Cliffs, New Jersey: Prentice-Hall, 1971. A compact, intense, and penetrating view of the Japanese "economic miracle."

Kaplan, Eugene J. *Japan: The Government-Business Relationship*. Washington: U.S. Government Printing Office, 1972. A helpful guide to this difficult subject.

Kobayashi, Shigeru. *Creative Management*. American Management Association, 1971. A unique human document by the former manager of Sony's Atsugi plant.

Maraini, Fosco. *Meeting with Japan*. New York: Viking, 1960. An ample, generous view of Japan and its people.

Morton, W. Scott. *Japan: Its History and Culture.* New York: Thomas Y. Crowell, 1975. A sensible overview.

Nakane, Chie. *Japanese Society.* Berkeley: University of California Press, 1970. The standard—and extremely wise—study of Japanese character and social psychology.

Rebischung, James. *Japan: The Facts of Modern Business and Social Life.* Tokyo: Charles E. Tuttle, 1974. A helpful short book.

Reischauer, Edwin O. *The United States and Japan.* New York: The Viking Press, 1950, 1973. An excellent analysis by the former United States ambassador to Japan.

Storry, Richard. *Japan.* London: Ernest Benn, Ltd., 1969. A helpful overview.

Talks and articles by Akio Morita

"Tradition Adapts to a Competitive Labor Market." *Columbia Journal of World Business,* Vol. III, No. 4, July-August 1968.
"International Marketing of Sony Corporation." Tokyo, July 14, 1969.
"What Distorts U.S.-Japan Relations." *Bungei Shunju,* February 1970.
"What Is the Difference Between the Japanese Management and the American?" Chicago, February 17, 1972.
"Human Elements in Japanese Business." Hakone, October 1, 1972.
"The Corporate Board of Directors in Japan." San Francisco, February 8, 1973.

"More Pleasurable 'My Own Golf' with Self-Designed, Hand-made Clubs of Uniform Length, Hammer-shaped for a Sure Hit." *Nihon Keizai Shibun,* August 24, 1973.

"The Free Economies—Which Way?" New York, November 13, 1973.

"Creativity in Modern Industry." Frank Nelson Doubleday Series, Smithsonian Institution, 1974.

"Management in Japan." In *Preparing Tomorrow's Business Leaders Today,* ed. Peter F. Drucker. Englewood Cliffs, New Jersey: Prentice-Hall, 1974.

Talk, Boston Security Analysts Society. February 19, 1975.

"Decision-Making in Japanese Business." Manila, September 30, 1975.

Talk, New York Society of Security Analysts. February 19, 1976.

Newspaper and Periodical Articles
Many news and magazine articles have appeared on Sony since the early 1960s; these are some of the more important commentaries, arranged chronologically.

"Sony—Japanese Industrial Miracle." J. D. Ratcliff. *The Lion,* July-August 1963; reprinted in *Reader's Digest.* The first major article on Sony in an American magazine, and extremely valuable for its details about Sony's early days.

"Sony's Purposeful Dreams." *Fortune,* July 1964.

"Horatio Alger Story—with a Japanese Twist." Jerrold L. Schecter. *The New York Times* Sunday Magazine, September 10, 1967.

"How to Get Bigger with Smaller Products." *Business Week,* May 25, 1968.

"Sony's Cofounder's Drive to Westernization Pays Off in Facing Competition Challenges." Scott R. Schmedel. *The Wall Street Journal,* November 18, 1969.

"Sony Executive Tunes in on the U.S." Robert E. Bedingfield. *The New York Times,* September 27, 1970.

"Japan, Inc.: Winning the Most Important Battle." *Time,* May 10, 1971.

"How Sony's One-Gun Color TV works." Len Buckwalter. *Electronics Illustrated,* March 1972.

"The Americanization of Sony." Gerd Wilcke. *The New York Times,* March 18, 1973.

"Japan." *Electronics,* November 22, 1973.

"Akio Morita/ of Sony Corp." *Nation's Business,* December 1973. An especially interesting (and long) interview with Morita.

"Made in America (under Japanese Management)." Richard Tanner Johnson and William G. Ouchi. *Harvard Business Review,* September-October 1974. An important, in-depth study of Japanese-based companies manufacturing in America.

"Sony Runs Its U.S. Plant the Japanese Way." *Business Week,* September 7, 1974.

"How Sony Developed Electronics for the World Market." Masaru Ibuka. *IEEE Transactions on Engineering Management,* Vol. EM-22, No. 1, February 1975. An invaluable and thorough account of the highlights of Sony.

"The Japanese Are Coming with Their Own Style of Management." Louis Kraar. *Fortune,* March 1975.

"The Ups and Downs of Sony Stock." John H. Allan. *The New York Times,* March 12, 1975.

"Mr. Transistor." Vincent Hanna. London Sunday *Times* Magazine, May 25, 1975. An ironic look at Morita in action.

"Video's New Frontier." *Newsweek,* December 8, 1975.

"No Excess Power to Protect Us." *Newsweek,* February 9, 1976. Interview with Morita by Bernard Krisher.

Index